THE CLOSING DOOR

DEE VAN BALEN

Copyright © 2010 Dee Van Balen
All rights reserved.

ISBN: 1452890722
ISBN-13: 9781452890722

Copyright Registration Number: TXu 1-614-152

DEDICATION

This book is dedicated to my sweet mother, for whom it was written. She was and continues to be my "Master of Life," as her positive influence has guided me through many storms.

The following verse from May Sarton's "The Invocation to Kali" was one of her favorites:
Help us to be the always hopeful
Gardeners of the spirit
Who know that without darkness
Nothing comes to birth
As without light
Nothing flowers

I also dedicate this book to my beautiful daughters, Ashley and Breean. Your support is unfailing, and you are and always will be a source of incredible love and inspiration for me. You are my own special blessings, my shining stars, and a light that feeds my soul. I love you so very much.

THE CLOSING DOOR

CHAPTERS:

1. THE BEGINNING 1
2. HALF-SMILE HAUNTING 13
3. DIFFERENT DOORS 23
4. SECONDS IN TIME. 33
5. BELIEVING IN MAGIC. 49
6. WALKING THROUGH LIFE. 55
7. THE ICY NIGHT 69
8. BIRTHS AND BLESSINGS 85
9. SLAMMING DOORS. 99
10. HILL STREET CLIMBING. 109
11. A BLESSING OR A CURSE. 121
12. THE OPEN GLASS DOOR. 131
13. YET TO COME .139

FOREWORD

In the period of 1940 to 1944, reported polio cases were eight in a hundred thousand; from 1945 to 1949, sixteen per hundred thousand; and from 1950 to 1954, twenty-five per hundred thousand, with the peak of thirty-seven per hundred thousand in 1952 (David M. Oshinsky, *Polio: An American Story* [New York: Oxford University Press, 2005])

Those of us who lived through that era remember the anxiety of every summer, as someone you knew was afflicted. This book is written by one such person. Her vivid recall is so exact that you too will feel the experience.

My own perspective is from two points of view: one as her friend for more than forty years and the other as the current CEO of The Watson Institute, the successor to the facility where the author spent her polio years.

Let her share her story with you.

Raymond B. White
Chief Executive Officer
The Watson Institute

PREFACE

The Closing Door was written in order to share a powerful story about a little girl who was separated from her family at a very young age and how it affected her personality and outlook on life.

Life is, however, a living book of stories. We are molded by our experiences and by the people who travel through life with us. We are forced to adjust our thinking and attitudes as we manage our personal paths of our lives. Reactions to and from our travels through time are what make us who we are.

CHAPTER 1
THE BEGINNING

CHAPTER ONE:
The Beginning

It was early evening as I imagined from my mind's eye at age five. She kissed me good night and rubbed my arm ever so gently, a mannerism she was known for. She then turned to walk toward the elevator doors that would steal her from me once again. She never looked back entering that elevator. She just stood still once inside, keeping her back to me until the doors closed.

I can still see this vision of my mother leaving each night. I can visualize the motion of my hospital room door closing...ever so slowly...ripping the comfort from my heart. The vacuum-pressure door seemed to tease me with the pain of what was to come. I was alone again. It was very still in my room then. An unsettling quiet crept in to greet me night after night after night.

It all began on a sunny spring day. I was running up a slight hill in our backyard toward my mother to give her a hug. I can see her standing there, a small-framed woman who radiated strength and love. Even then, I knew she was a "Master of Life." As I approached, she asked me a question that hangs in my mind to this day, a question that marked the beginning of a different kind of life. The question was, "Why are you limping?" It was shortly thereafter that my own door closed.

In my memories, the next moment after that fateful hill climb is that of my high-barred hospital bed in the D.T. Watson Home for Crippled Children.

Polio was Dr. Jonas Salk's diagnosis. It was a form of polio that affected my right hip. (Even now, I sometimes find myself in awe of the fact that Dr. Salk — *the* Dr. Salk — had anything to do with my history and my hospital stay.) Though I am lucky enough to walk without a physical limp, I carry with me many remnants of that disease. So many memories of my stay at the D.T. Watson Home — which then and now I think of simply as "The Home" — are engrained in my mind and have molded my personality. I still get tears in my eyes when I visualize the memory of my mother leaving me at night, alone to face the darkness. I can still see clearly the view from the only window in my room and the view of my body, from the chest down, lying in that bed. Though I was just five years old when I entered The Home, the memories are fresh.

In one of medicine's great ironies, the treatment for this paralyzing disease was to, in essence, paralyze me. Traction was applied to my right leg, and I was to be totally non-weight-bearing for one year. My tiny body rested on a slanted, padded wooden board, and the traction attachment stayed wrapped around my right ankle for an entire year. The high bars that surrounded my bed obstructed my view, but I could still see out of the window at the foot of my bed. My magical window!

Though I came to dread those lonely nights, I found hope in the mornings. I would awaken wondering what would happen that day, looking forward to the things that might be different and taking comfort in the knowledge that my mother would be coming. I knew that after my bed-bath and breakfast, soon it would be the moment when my mother would arrive. She always greeted me with such joy, and I know her love helped me to heal. She was and remains the most beautiful sight I have ever seen.

I didn't measure time like others. The light through my window was my clock, the changing seasons my calendar. The nurses were loud and busy in the halls, but I trained my ears to find the sounds from outside my window. The birds' good morning songs were a special greeting just for me. The raindrops became musical notes as they pitter-pattered onto my windowsill.

The snow meant another season had arrived and another change would break the monotony of my view. I smiled and listened and watched time pass by. I knew that after my breakfast it would be closer to the moment that my mother would arrive to greet me with her beautiful healing face of hope and her infectious smile. Her smile told me without words that everything would be all right and that soon I would be home again with my family. With countless hours to think and imagine, I began a process of "mind managing" that would see me through many difficult days ahead.

The days continued to pass in three main chunks of time: "before my mother's visit," "during my mother's visit," and "after my mother's visit." It was a very long year, but the changes of seasons also changed my mind and the direction of my thinking. Another dynamic sequence of profound memories happened during my snowy season at The Home. It was Christmastime and joy was in the air. It was a new change and another reason to believe. When my door opened I could see the lights lining the hallway, and they sparkled as if they were put there purposely to change moods. Those shimmering lights certainly changed me, and the thoughts of Santa arriving changed me too. I believed, and that belief helped the days go by quickly as I anticipated his arrival. This was a gift I didn't realize I was receiving, but it was a gift nonetheless.

But the biggest gift of all that year was brought about because of my father. My family owned a dry cleaning and laundry business, and we had many large trucks. My father asked permission to take me home for one night: Christmas Eve. My family wanted me to be with them on Christmas morning. My father explained that they could roll me up into one of the trucks, secure my hospital bed, and drive safely to my real home. The staff at The Home agreed to the plan. A new door would soon open for me, and it would be me leaving on that elevator instead of my mother!

The arrangements were made, and the night before my departure, I was moved into a magnificent ballroom with high ceilings, huge windows, and marvelous wood-paneled walls. I assumed then that they moved me to make it easier for my transport. I wonder now if the real reason for moving us "lucky few" to the ballroom at night was so the other children who were not able to go home wouldn't see us leave.

There were many crying children in that room — and I was one of them. This new change was a little frightening; I still felt alone even though other children were there with me. But I had never seen any of them before, so I felt uncomfortable, and it was hard for me

The Closing Door

to fall asleep. All I could do was try to control what I was thinking about, and that's what I did.

I watched the beautiful snowfall outside the large windows, and soon the room became quiet. Those windows seemed as magical as the one in my room. I stared out of them and thought about seeing my family the next day. Those thoughts calmed me, and so did the view. The spotlights outside made the snowflakes glitter, and it was as if the flakes were marking the time for me. One... two...three. No, one...two...three. I couldn't count them, they moved so fast! It was hard to track their fall, as they changed directions quickly, just like life.

The next thing I knew, it was morning, and my moment had arrived. I was thrilled to see my older brothers. They sensed I was nervous for the travel, and they laughed with me to ease my anxiety. They rolled my stretcher up into the truck, secured it, and off we went. We drove toward home, over the bridge and to the place that was truly where I lived. My heart felt so full and it was almost overwhelming when we pulled up to the home that housed our family of eight. Home at last! They'd made a "WELCOME HOME!" sign and hung it over the front steps. There was a lot of excitement and many happy faces. Everyone looked over or through the hospital bed rails to say hello. It was a glorious moment, and it was not strange at all, as the family web had already begun knitting us close as no others. It was a true family bond.

I felt comfortable even though I didn't live there anymore. They rolled my hospital bed up planks on our front steps, into our house and then our dining room. The mantel was decorated beautifully. I kept starring at the fireplace, already nervous for Santa's arrival. I cried because I was afraid Santa would slide down and see only me. My father's voice was a security in itself, and his presence my relief. But it was my sweet mother who slept on the floor beside me all night, and I slept knowing she was in charge.

I don't remember anything that transpired after the moment I fell asleep. Interesting, isn't it? I am sure Christmas morning was exciting, and I assume they would have rolled my bed into the hallway so I could be with everyone while they opened their gifts. We always set up a huge Christmas tree in the corner of the living room, but I don't remember seeing it that year. I cannot figure out how these memories got erased. I do know that I don't remember leaving to go back to The Home, but I am certain I put this particular "block" in place because I didn't want to remember the pain of leaving. This behavioral defense mechanism developed by me at this early age was unplanned, but it worked for the most part.

This method of managing is still very much a part of me. I find myself searching for the bright side of negative situations in order to make my moments in time more manageable. I can erase many of the negative memories I experience as if they never existed. This method has helped me through many traumas throughout my life, and as my story unfolds, you will see how.

I am sure returning to The Home was traumatic for me, but at the time, I didn't know those memories would be erased from my mind. I know now that it was one of the reasons I was determined to have the skill to open any door that was closing on me. It was a silent type of protection.

In my opinion, the D.T. Watson Home was a happy place filled with sincere people who truly cared about the patients who lived there. This feeling that hovered over The Home was felt by all, I assume. At least I felt it. I believe the security that resulted from this feeling contributed to my healing — as well as how often I had to erase bad memories. Considering the circumstances, The Home was more than just a hospital focused on healing. It was everyone's home away from home. They must have had tricks of their own for managing all of us. For instance, I remember the lights being dim a lot of the time. Perhaps it was so we could sleep more and pass the time away.

It is strange how many ways there are to trick time. I know now and I knew then that my mind is a powerful tool.

I can't remember how long it was before a new therapy was introduced. I know that one day they removed me from traction and

The Closing Door

placed me on a stretcher without weights attached to my leg. They opened my hospital door, and we traveled halls I had never seen before. Unfamiliar faces stared at me, wondering who I was as well. When they opened a new door, I was surprised to see a huge swimming pool! They gently wheeled me onto a ramp, stretcher and all, into warm water that was supposed to be the next step to recovery. They eased me into the water little by little; the warm water covered me gradually. It was magnificent!

The water felt soothing and helped my nervousness subside. They moved my leg and I could feel the odd sensation I almost had forgotten. I hadn't been in water for almost a year, and I will never forget how wonderful it was to have the water surrounding me that day. This may be why I love to soak in a steaming hot tub each evening and why I love to swim. As long as I can remember, water has been my solace and my secret escape. It is and always will be a place where challenges seem to disappear and where peace fills my soul.

My water therapy was my favorite part of recovery, but I also looked forward to the nursing staff wheeling me out on a deck that was high above the grounds. I loved to gaze out over the land that surrounded The Home. It was well groomed and peaceful. The trees were plentiful and the wind seemed to play with the leaves. I used to be mesmerized watching the motion of the leaves. They would sway as if they were dancing. It is amazing how nature tells its own story.

The staff made the time move quickly with their gentle ways and caring hearts. This genuine caring was so real! I remember one nurse, though, who was not a positive force on our floor. She was not happy with herself, and her voice sent chills down my spine. She had very strong hands and she seemed to do everything quickly and without facial expression. I didn't like it when she was working. This nurse was heavy on her feet and quite strict. I can still hear her yelling at us to go to sleep and to stop talking. I wonder if she is one of the reasons I talk so much. My roommate and I always still whispered after she left our room.

One night I was unhooked from my traction because I had just had a bed bath. The hospital bed's sidebar was down, and the nurse left the room for a few minutes. I whispered to my roommate that I knew I could now walk and that I would show her. She said I shouldn't try…but of course I did it anyway.

The hope the two of us felt was so powerful that it alone should have allowed me to walk. I stood on one leg and we looked at each other, smiling with the anticipation of success. I took one step and fell to the floor. Our loud, giant nurse came running in and put me back into my bed and my traction. She was so mad — and I was so frightened. I was strapped down so I wouldn't get out again, at least not on her shift. It was a long night without sleep.

The moment in time my friend and I shared was wonderful. The hope of being healed was one of the powers we had within us, and that hope made us believe we would both be healed one day. We shared that room for a short time, as she was much sicker than I was. I don't remember her name, and I can't remember the day she left. Another mind block.

My days were filled with steps toward recovery. The exercises were tiring but necessary. My mother made it easier with her smile and her confidence. She used to be so calm, and her beautiful smile was in itself healing for me. She was a nurse by trade and a perfect mother. I don't know what I would have done without her. I now know why she never turned around to face me after she got into the elevator to leave each night — and that she sobbed as she drove home.

Soon I was fitted with a metal brace that was connected to high-topped brown orthopedic shoes. A set of tiny wooden crutches were to be my new support system. I was taken down to the physical therapy floor so they could stand me up for the first time since I entered The Home.

The huge hallway outside the foyer of The Home was the exact spot where I suddenly went from laying flat to being in an upright position. When it happened, I stood motionless, smiling. This position seemed natural to be in even though it had been almost a year since I had last stood upright. I will never forget that hall! Everything looked different when I was standing.

Each day, I worked toward walking again. The therapists and nurses would tell me over and over again to just tell my foot to step forward. Were they kidding? My foot wasn't listening to me. I tried and tried, but I just stood still. They said, "Think about it moving forward just a little bit." I did. IT DID NOT!

We tried and tried day after day, but it seemed my first step would never happen. I didn't give up and then…one day it worked! I remember that I concentrated so hard as I stared down at my foot that I felt like I willed it to move. I will never forget that moment! It did finally listen to me!

Certainly, I know now that all of the physical therapy had awakened my muscles. But I still believe that it was mostly because I made it move with my mind. It was my own miracle of sorts, another blessing I received and still smile about.

That second seemed to last a lifetime — but my family was not there to share it. I wonder why they didn't arrange for my parents to come and watch me. Perhaps because they knew it would take a long time for me to walk again. But I had won, and I knew one day I would be able to run into the wind and be steady on my feet, free of any apparatus supporting me.

I was one of the lucky children, though, because even then I knew that some of the little people who shared The Home would not win their battles. There were many levels of illness in these crippled children. Some of them could hardly sit up in their wheelchairs. Very sad! I remember looking up and seeing some of the other children smiling at me. Their eyes told me they were sharing in my success. I smiled back at them as if to say *I hope you step forward too.* This nonverbal communication was another step toward all of our healing. It was another profound example of our faith.

It was very bittersweet when I had my magical moment of success because within seconds I felt sadness overcome me. I knew that many of the children there with me would never be able to walk, and I think they knew it too. So when I looked up after my foot moved forward and into their faces, my euphoric expression became masked and my smile took on a different form by choice because I didn't want to hurt anyone's feelings.

You see…I changed my smile. I did it on purpose, and it made my experience go into a new level. I learned at that moment that it was the right decision to make — and I noticed their expressions change as well. It seemed as if they had a new sparkle in their eyes, and that sparkle seemed to say that we could all still have hope and believe. That made me feel good. A different kind of happiness entered my heart. I felt like my first step not only made me happy, it made them happy too. For just a moment, I felt I helped uplift hearts.

I knew that one day soon I would be returning home and many of them would not. I also knew I was thrilled that I had taken my first step since I'd been placed in traction, and my heart was filled with joy. But I could feel the pain of others who were probably never going to be able to leave — and so we shared in the "Half-Smile Haunting."

CHAPTER 2
HALF-SMILE HAUNTING

CHAPTER TWO:
Half-Smile Haunting

This was the beginning of my "Half Smile," and the haunting began to unfold. It wasn't a negative phrase but a positive one. It was and still is a natural managing tactic for me. Like a dimmer light switch that can be turned down to fit a mood or an experience. It is my personal "dimming" mode. The Half Smile is an emotional check and balance system used for self-protection! A mind-altering defense mechanism that is an unrehearsed response to a situation, and one that comes straight from the heart. Like a safety net for the soul, or even multiple souls. It provides a private sort of healing and a type of escape. For those of us together at The Home, it was our *magic* and our magnetic force that drew us together like no others.

Yes, my first step was glorious! A personal accomplishment that filled my soul with joy, and I "dimmed" my expression for the moment. The patients shared this secret power in The Home. It was a power of sharing hope and exchanging positive glances for encouragement.

Another way of explaining the Half Smile could be found in the smiles my mother and I shared after she kissed me good night before leaving. Her beautiful smile gave me peace, and I would sleep through the night knowing that one day I would be home again. I smiled at her so she would not worry about me. I knew she didn't want to leave, and she knew I didn't want her to go. And we both used the Half Smile for healing. It was our way of protecting ourselves — and each other.

My developing level of sensitivity was growing rapidly but unnoticed, at least by me. The experiences I had and my interactions with other children like me created a molding of silent expression and a different aspect to my personality. I didn't like to be alone and I felt uncomfortable about people leaving me because of my experiences in The Home. But the Half Smile helped me get

The Closing Door

through the long nights, and I had learned to control that. I could look to myself for strength.

During those days, many doors were closing — but at the same time, many of them were opening! I had a new support system. I was standing tall with those new crutches and brace, and soon I would be the master of them.

Eventually I was strong enough to be discharged. A new patient would live in my room, and the walls that surrounded that child would no longer belong to me. That vacuum-pressure door would no longer shut me in and leave me alone in the dark.

My ownership of the Half Smile was a silent blessing for my soul while I was young, and it carried me throughout my life in a positive way. This chapter is titled "Half-Smile Haunting" because of how many times I had to use the Half Smile! I had to use it over and over because there were still years ahead of us that we had to travel back up that long hill so I could be fitted for a new brace. Each trip meant I still was not healed and my nightmare continued.

The pinching action of the bracket on my brace has left a tiny scar on the inside of my right leg. When I look at this tiny scar, I am reminded of how this apparatus held me up. The scar is a reminder of my own lesson learned: to believe. I am grateful that the result was success, as many stories do not have the same ending. But my experience certainly opened a new window of understanding. I continue to search for strength to help me stay up like those uncomfortable crutches and brace. The sweet older man who used to measure me knew all about the methods of the Half Smile — he used it well!

Someone once asked me if my parents ever discussed my prognosis or the fact that I might not get better, and I said no. I'd never even thought about that before. It is very strange, but I believe my age had a lot to do with how they handled it. They were very positive, and any prognosis other than me being healed was just wasn't an option. Of course I would get better and walk.

Dee Van Balen

In my family, we were all taught that steps were not for standing on, but for climbing! Therefore, my time in The Home would end and normalcy would return — and that was that. There were six children in our family and a lot of action. I think back to those times shared with many, and I can honestly say that I do not remember anyone ever fighting. People don't believe me when I say that, but it is true. There was always so much going on among all of our lives that no one spent time bothering to get into any sibling rivalries. We just supported each other, and the love continued to flow like water, molding us together as one.

I believe in my heart that concentrating on what happened to me wasn't a topic for discussion because of this phenomenon. This was a blessing, as I didn't feel left out or different. I carried this attitude with me and that is probably why I cannot think of horrific emotional trauma connected to my "crippled time."

I have a very positive outlook and am able to find my way through life's darkness when it falls on me. I attribute this to the growth I experienced then, and to the people who walked through life with me during that time and held me up. They gave me an inner peace and added strength I needed for my soul. They gave me a secret crutch for support so I could face any new negatives that would come my way. I am grateful because their interactions with me made those years a profound learning experience, as they sheltered me from my own fears while I went through it.

As I got older, I started to jot down feelings about my stay at the D.T. Watson Home and how it affected me and my view of life. The Home is still a place I like to visit, particularly during challenging times. I have often found myself driving up there on my own, just to gaze out over the beautiful land and try to remember the power we all have inside of us. It is my way of getting back into focus. You see, I took from there an inner peace that resulted from my accomplishments there. I didn't leave The Home with anything but the power I had obtained from spending time there. It was a personal power I felt inside my soul; it was a growth that, at the time, I didn't realize was happening to me or how it would change my life.

The Closing Door

As I began to put my puzzle together, I found that I had never thought about many facets of my "crippled time." Someone once asked me if my brothers and sisters felt resentment toward me since I had to have so much attention during that time. I just stared at the person with a blank look on my face. I can honestly say that I never thought about that either — so I asked.

The answers I received were exactly what I thought they would be. No, they did not resent me. They were just happy I was getting better and glad I was home again. It's possible they had never thought about that topic either. Many managing tactics were in effect for all of us to learn from, I guess. I wish my mother were alive today so I could ask her how she handled that topic with each of her children. I don't know which words she chose to explain what was happening, but she obviously chose the correct ones.

Another piece of my puzzle was connected to our family pediatrician, Dr. Nix, who was a friend of Dr. Salk's. My mother was familiar with the "Pioneer Polio Research" that Dr. Salk was working on, and both doctors discussed the research with her. Mother was a registered nurse, and she believed in the work they were doing to prevent polio. When Dr. Salk approached her in the hospital and asked her if she would be willing to have a few of her children participate in the program, she said yes. She registered my two oldest brothers and my oldest sister in the program. Children had to be at least five years old to participate.

I am amazed when I think about the fact that they were part of that discovery. It is also very scary to think about the possibility of it not working. Talk about having to use the Half Smile!

They all feel very proud that they actually helped with the finding and success of the polio vaccine. All three of them still remember the many children lined up, waiting for their shots — and they all agree that the orange juice they had to drink following the shot was gross. However, my oldest brother is still upset that he had to be one of these "Polio Pioneers." He was much older, and I can only assume he looked at the testing through different eyes because of his age. They were frightened eyes, and his mind still holds negative memories so many years later.

It's not that he didn't want to help, but it upsets him that he didn't have a choice. It disturbs him when the subject comes up. "What if something had gone wrong?" he wonders. He says our mother's decision to assist was a great decision because it worked. He trusted her and believed it would work, even back then, but it still bothers him.

He says it is amazing to think about how many children were saved from this crippling disease, and that is what is important. But he also says that if he were asked to give his children to participate in research for a new vaccine, he wouldn't.

We all have different experiences that are our own life lessons. Whether the experiences are happy or sad, they all teach us. We learn from everything that happens to us. It is part of our self-discovery and the molding of our minds. It all boils down to the mastering abilities of personal managing. This is something that is ongoing, as the new situations we encounter change just like the hands of a clock. Time moves forward even when we don't want it to. "Ticking time and managing moments." We all need to know our strengths — and we need to recognize our weaknesses in order to rise above our challenges. I am still working on my self-discovery, and I continue to use my past as a positive crutch to propel me forward into my future.

My Half Smile allowed me to get through many rough times, but I never got used to the "Haunting."

"Life is, however, a living book of stories." I make mention of this in my prologue, and I wanted to highlight it again because we are molded by our experiences and by the people who travel through life with us. We are forced to adjust our thinking and our attitudes as we manage the personal paths of our lives. We use many different methods of managing. These methods are the result of the many lessons that others present to us, and they assist us in our growth.

The Closing Door

I was forced to adjust my thinking as well as my attitude toward my situation in order to manage the personal path I faced. Our reactions to what happens to us make us who we are. I am grateful for the fact that I had a loving family with me during my "crippled time" and thankful for all of those who cared for me in The Home. I think of them as my "Adjusters."

My Adjusters were all positive people, and they were the forces that picked up my spirit when it was down. They groomed me, so to speak, enabling me to see life as a glass half full, not half empty. I have shared many of the different areas in which they have all helped me while I suffered alone. Each muscle I use to smile was strengthened by each one of them. I didn't frown much, I was told.

I have chosen to dedicate my book of life to my sweet mother, my Master of Life. She is the main positive force that has always been with me. My mother and father were always my life teachers. My father is a powerful man, and I adore him. He still "grounds" me.

Parents make a difference. My mother's "Master" was her mother. My grandmother was a very strong woman with much power. Not the kind of power that can build cities, but a power within her that built strong hearts. She was an endless giver of love and a gentle woman that people listened to. She had many messages. She faced many rocky roads when she was young, but managed basically on her own and succeeded. She looked to the heavens for her strength and found it. "He" was the one who held her up.

There is sunshine behind every cloud, and storms do settle eventually. I believe that a person who chooses to develop optimism will have a better outlook on life. If and when a challenge we are facing does not end up as we had hoped, that is when we should spend time regrouping and adjust accordingly. We would waste less time in the negative, an area that is not a happy place for anyone to be. We do not need to go there. The "negative space" in life is a dark place where smiles are missing; negative energy affects not only the person in that space, but all of those around him or her. It brings everyone down. Maybe it is easier for pessimists to be pessimistic because they fear failure. I say accept failure when it comes. Have hope always and believe. If you think you can, you usually can. The peace you possess during the challenge by being positive makes all challenges seem smaller. Have hope and know that the light is always stronger than the dark.

I hope my story will help others to have hope and to believe that there is sunshine behind clouds and that the storms we go through settle and bring new life into the world. I know many others have been through much harder times and, yes, some of their traumas have not had happy endings. This fact breaks my heart. I hope that while you travel with me through time, you will find some peace in your heart from your own past that you have forgotten, and that it rekindles the joy in your heart. I hope you too are blessed by having positive people in your life who walk with you every step of the way.

We all have a story. This is just mine.

CHAPTER 3
DIFFERENT DOORS

CHAPTER THREE:
Different Doors

As you know, the title of my book is *The Closing Door*. I refer to the closing door as one that shut me out and locked me in. Its reference is a tremendous positive power that taught me that the "door," even though it closed each night and left me alone in a room without love, would indeed open again, bringing new light and a restored comfort to my heart. I learned that even though I was experiencing pain in my heart and a fear of being alone, the new day would come and the door would open again, bringing with it my mother to visit. This made my time in The Home, high up on that hill, easier to deal with, although I didn't know it at the time. I know this method of managing now only because I am an adult. I get it!

I still think about that damn door! My mind wonders about it and compares situations to all of the different types of doors that are available to us these days. I'll bet most people can relate any time of their lives to a particular door that fits. There are so many types of doors to choose from. There are doors that are wooden and doors that are steel. There are screen doors and storm doors and Dutch doors that open up in halves. These Dutch doors are the types of doors that allow emotions to escape from the top and hold them in by the bottom half...kind of like the Half Smile!

A great man named D.T. Watson opened many doors for many people. His dream of building a home for crippled children to live in and be taken care of came true. I would have liked this man, and I believe we would have gotten along very well.

D.T. Watson was a very interesting man. Anyone who ever had the opportunity to meet him was blessed. He was a hard worker and a visionary. He was born in the village of Washington, Pennsylvania, on January 2, 1844, in the vicinity of Canonsburg, Pennsylvania. Wanting to learn more about him, I read *D.T. Watson of Counsel* (Francis R. Harbison, Pittsburgh: Davis & Warde, 1945). This book

The Closing Door

was so interesting! Harbison wrote, "David Thompson Watson was recognized as one of the English-speaking world's great lawyers and as one of the two greatest in his era. But in the inner circles of his profession he was the Sir Galahad of the Bar...His name became synonymous with personal and professional integrity and with professional ethics; and his escutcheon, etched with his code, 'do justly, love mercy and walk humbly with thy God,' remained unsullied." (p. 3)

I would have loved to have had the opportunity to meet this man.

After I finished the book, I sat thinking about how much his love and caring ways for others affected so many. He was a famous man of many talents with a sensitive, caring wife as well. Together they willed the institute for the D.T. Watson Home. It was a brilliant plan, and one that is still developing today. The old face of the original building has not changed. When I viewed it recently, many of the memories came flooding back and it felt as though I had just left there.

It is uncanny that, as Harbison wrote, "Watson's superlative expression for the highest, the worthiest ideals in his profession was the 'mountain-top ways.' Again and again he used the expression. He said to a Bar Association, 'We should look to the mountain tops, not to the valleys, up where the air is clearer, purer and more bracing. It gives you nobler, better thoughts and aims.'" (p. 247)

When I read this, I thought it was perfect that Watson chose to live high in the hills of Sewickley, Pennsylvania. It is a place where he could live and feel the breeze of nature and think clearly. It was the location where eventually he would build and house many little children in need. High up on a hill where indeed the birds would sing proudly and the view would be so magnificent. It was almost like a secret venue for healing for all those who lived and worked there.

The Watson estate was named "Sunny Hill," and named appropriately. The original stone wall that surrounds the grounds is still intact. There is a cottage, known as the Gate-Keeper's Lodge, built in English style just as you enter the estate, and the road that leads to The Home has beautiful trees that hover over it like a serene tunnel.

D.T. Watson planned the development of the lands just as precisely as he planned for his Home for Crippled Children. The land was beautiful and well kept, offering serenity to all those who visited. Many new buildings have been erected in order to continue the development of The Home. His vision of helping patients and giving care to those in need is still functioning today. Yes...Mr. D.T. Watson opened doors!

I don't remember the day I left The Home for good. I don't remember coming home to my family. I do remember being the only one who couldn't wear fancy shoes and that I had to wear a brace and use crutches for many years to come. It isn't a bad memory, though. Once again, the support and love from my family made the healing time go quickly, and being different wasn't too much of a challenge.

"Life is not easy," my parents preached. The attitude that one adopts opens windows of happiness and enables one to stay on an optimistic path. Like any map, sharp turns occur and can change your life forever. Some of the best paths are full of rocks and are hard to follow — but the view is beautiful.

I have mentioned two brilliant men who indeed opened many doors. D.T. Watson opened the doors for care and discovery. His wife shared in his mission and demonstrated this by being supportive and instrumental in the development of The Home. She was an artist and creative in her own expression.

Dr. Jonas Salk opened his mind to discovery at a young age, spending more time reading and applying learned knowledge into science and life. The "Calling to Find a Cure" interview by the Academy of Achievement (16 May 1991, www.achievement.org/ autodoc/page/sal0int-1) gives many insights into Salk's personal and professional history. I was not surprised to find that he was driven by a desire to make a difference in the world, but I found it

The Closing Door

interesting that, in many ways, he was a self-taught man. He was not classically trained as a scientist, but he relied on his medical training and scientific mind and followed his intuition in developing the polio vaccine. His thinking was unconventional, and he faced much doubt and criticism within the medical and scientific communities. But he was not to be deterred.

I found many of his insights and assertions to be both logical and profound. This was a truly brilliant and inspiring man! He spoke of balancing knowledge and wisdom; trusting your intuition when reason doesn't provide all the answers; and the important role of "evolvers," those who are not content simply to maintain the status quo. I was impressed by the confidence in his words and his strong sense of self, and I connected with his belief that we all need to find our purpose in life and embrace it.

But I was particularly struck by the enormous respect he had for his wife, Françoise. This man who changed modern medicine actually marveled in his wife's intellect and her artistic abilities. He mentioned a book dedication to her in which he referred to her as "someone who illuminates all life." I have tremendous respect for the fact that he placed such value on his private world even while being mindful of serving the world outside of himself. What a fantastic achievement!

Dr. Salk had a calling to find many cures. Obviously, his development of the polio vaccine changed the world and made an incredible difference. But I feel deep in my soul that, above and beyond all his success in the field of medical science, his grasp on life is perhaps the greatest gift he had to give. I share his belief in the importance of "life skills" and the need for all individuals to believe in themselves. I also agree with his feeling that we all have personal power that needs to be nurtured. We should all try to build each other's self-understanding and awareness. Too many times, opportunities arise where we miss the chance to give the positive to others.

It is very odd that the history of these two great men was not my focus of interest until later in life, after the experience that I had high up on that hill. Once again, only after years of facing many different types of challenges did the thought start to creep into my mind. Only as an adult did the interest evolve as I started to decipher the reasons why I looked at life as I did and still do. It is all very easy to see as I look at the big picture now. I still am filled with wonder, and my research and personal discovery is only starting to break into this new life adventure.

Other than family and friends, a focal point in my life is my belief in God and the stability that is open for all of us to take if we just believe. My door has always been able to open and close, knowing deep in my heart that above it all is a force that is stronger than I am and ready to walk through life *with* me...not beside me!

The serenity prayer has always brought me solace, and many verses left behind in written form from my mother and her mother — which I read often — give me the little extra edge I need to keep me moving forward in the right direction and frame of mind. It is with all of this that I chose to share my thoughts about my life and the people who helped guide me along the way. They were all my scientists and visionaries in their own space, reaching out to me and all others in need. My strength was in the fact that I believed in the staff that helped me through my illness, my friends I met along the way, my family, and my God. That is power.

It doesn't matter where people grow up or what type of history precedes them, the opportunity to rise from it all is a reality. Let the people who surround you seep into your life and allow their positive influence to direct you. All levels of life can feel love and have love. It is there for the taking. Confusion and conflict shade the view and stop some people from seeing it. A little bit of openness can let in the light and renew souls. The power within can then start to emerge, and greater steps of the positive will begin to be noticed.

Soon none of these influential people would be a part of my life anymore. No staff nurse would awaken me for any reason, nor would anyone see me on my crutches walking the hall. My time at the D.T. Watson Home for Crippled Children was coming to an end.

The Closing Door

They had completed their job and it was time for me to step forward out of the front doors of The Home and into the life of my family once again.

The days became longer as the time for me to leave got closer. I didn't lose my ability to trick time, though; in my mind, it was now just the ticking of the clock! The excitement of it finally happening became overwhelming. My little birds on the windowsill still sang, but I didn't pay as much attention to their songs. The reality clock was in charge. And I was going home!

Many hospitals have professionals who prepare people for this transition. I remember one time that this type of situation applied — and it was one that didn't end well. That's probably why I remember it! I think I was a good patient most of the time. At least that is how I remember my behavior. I know this wasn't the case one evening, when they put me in a wheelchair and rolled me down the hall to eat dinner in a small kitchen. I guess it was their way of enabling me to have a change of scenery as well as reintroduce me to a regular kitchen.

I had never been rolled down to the right outside of my room, and the trip was a little scary. The "mean nurse" was in charge of my ride — another likely reason that I remember this evening. Once we were inside, she rolled my wheelchair up to a table and set a plate of food in front of me. I was by myself in that room.

I thought that it was also odd that I was the only one there, but the excitement of a new environment was interesting to me. I felt like it was almost kind of fun...until she shut the door and left. I kept wondering why people kept shutting doors and leaving.

Another reason I remember this event is because the vegetable I was supposed to eat was spinach. I hated spinach! The mean nurse kept coming into this "kitchen," telling me to eat my spinach and that I had to sit there until I did. Then she would leave again, closing the door behind her. This went on for quite a long time. As a five-year-old, I thought it seemed like hours. Prior to this moment, the only truly "bad behavior" I ever displayed in The Home was when I got out of bed and tried to walk. The spinach was about to add another moment of bad behavior!

I wanted to go back to my room, so after multiple checks by the nurse, I decided when she left the next time I would make sure it would be her last! I took the spinach into my tiny right hand and quickly threw it under the table, and it landed on the floor and close to the wall. I was nervous waiting for her return, as I couldn't get out of my wheelchair to pick up the spinach and return it to my plate. I prayed that she wouldn't notice it was on the floor, and I remember wishing that the spinach was a different color so it could blend in with the floor.

When the nurse came back in, she was so proud of me because my plate was empty, and she told me so. I looked at her face with fright in my eyes but a crooked smile on my face that I hoped she didn't notice. I knew it was not a very nice thing to do, but I simply did not want to eat that spinach! And I certainly wasn't going to confess. Approximately thirty minutes later she came stomping into my room, yelling at me for my action. I deserved it. And funny enough, I like spinach now.

But this negative experience taught me a lesson. I think that perhaps this "mean nurse" was actually an instrument of peace. That maybe she was the one who erased the tiny fear I was holding in my heart over facing another change, turning my fear into a desire to run to just to get away from her...even if it was on crutches!

I remember walking down the hall without assistance instead of being rolled down on a stretcher to the familiar deck overlooking The Home's grounds. It was magnificent! Perfect trees in a pattern, with a calmness about it that anyone could feel. It was enough to improve moods and alter attitudes.

D.T. Watson was brilliant! He knew that it would be like that because he planned it that way. A place up high on the hills where fresh air would enable clearer thinking, and the beauty of it all would encompass all that he had dreamed would happen. Healing

The Closing Door

bodies and mending hearts for all who had physical challenges and needed help.

The home that he built for crippled children was a great success, and I am only one little girl who lived his dream.

I pray that all of the doors that you have opened continue to open up for more new discoveries and ideas that will change our future. Thank you, D.T. Watson!

CHAPTER 4
SECONDS IN TIME

CHAPTER FOUR:
Seconds in Time

I was home at last, but the crutches by my sides and the brace that was on my right leg still were a part of me. A new door of life was now opened, but it was a familiar door that I walked through.

I reentered my family life changed. I was a year older, but because of what had happened to me, I was much older in my mind. Most people can't even remember anything about when they were five years old. I didn't know it then, but I was not the typical six-year-old when I came home, and the weight that I carried with me wasn't only from my crutches.

I slept in my own bed and it felt like new. I could see my sister's face as she laid still and slept the whole night through. I, however, didn't sleep much that first night home. I felt comfortable, but it was different. I didn't have the high, shiny metal bars surrounding me, and I felt like I might fall out. I felt secure but not totally. I knew I didn't have to worry this time about Santa seeing only me because it wasn't the season. I knew that my parents were sleeping in a room not far away, but it still felt odd. Thought it felt good to know that the mean nurse wouldn't be waking me!

I was a happy child with the people around me that continued to stabilize me. I had spent the last year of my young life adjusting time to fit my schedule. I had been tricking the clock, so to speak, and my seconds moved faster as a result of it. My family, however, made the seconds valuable with their constant love and caring ways. They were the battery behind my numbers and all of the "seconds" that passed within my year in the home seemed faster because of them. Ah, time...

As my story unfolds, it is important to know that the "clock" that ran our home was one that ticked loudly. There were eight people who lived in our house. We each had our own personalities but bonded together easily on a daily basis. This bond was like a clock that was perfectly set, and it never skipped a beat with the strength of the love around it. Certainly there were times that it needed to be "fixed" or there were times when it needed to be adjusted, but our clock worked and my mother was there to make sure that it never was truly broken.

The day I ran up the hill to kiss my sweet mother was a moment in time that nothing could have changed.

I have spent time thinking about that one second in time, and I am amazed when I think about what was happening to everyone in that second. I know that many people were experiencing much more difficult situations than I was, but many of them were smiling due to a beautiful event that occurred.

I couldn't change my second, but I wonder how many people could have changed theirs. Seconds count.

My mother didn't ever want to stop the clock. She believed that our time here on earth had a purpose, and she used her time well. She was a master of managing. She always told us to make good use of our time and to set our goals high. She believed that no matter what situation occurred — whether it was good or bad — there was a reason behind it. She believed that eventually we would realize that positive things occur even through bad times. It was growth in different directions. She traveled all of our rocky roads with us, and as it turns out, she was correct. I have been able to find positive things that happened to me while I was crippled, so she was right. She was very wise as well as beautiful. Everyone could see that she had a heart of gold, and she would go out of her way to help anyone. I truly believe that she touched many of the lives of others outside of our family because of these qualities, and I was always proud that she was my mother.

In the front of this book, there is a portion of one of her favorite poems, and it was one of the lessons that she taught us. She believed that it was important to be gardeners of others' spirits. She taught us to make a difference and to help others when they need it.

She also said that giving is better than receiving and that moods change for the better when you take time for others. All of these qualities made her a true "Gardener of the Spirit."

"Seconds in time." I have stressed the idea of time. We have many different instruments to measure it. Mine was simply "tricking time," but there are stopwatches for timing performance, a world clock that has different times that are indicative for positions in the universe, and stylish watches that have changed with time. We have many choices of how we want to know exactly what time it is. Our seconds count.

Life is what it is. Whatever we have done during the time of growing older we have done as a result of something, and only we can measure how well we spent our time. Our choices are our own and we must be responsible for the choices we make. We also have to take responsibility for our seconds in time, as we all have our own clocks.

What happens to us is our history. Our families are a very important part of our time, and they are memory-builders for each of us. I don't know what I would have done without my family. I know that my seconds in time while I was ill would have been much longer. They are the reason for my endless faith in life, and they all are the reason I continue to have hope. We had faith in each other, faith in life, and faith in love.

I struggled like the rest of the children my age with typical challenges that broke hearts and wounded egos. I always kept looking at the bright side of things, though, as nothing seemed harder than saying goodbye each night to my loving mother while I had been at The Home. My family kept me focused.

I think that all of the feelings I retained are powerful, and I truly believe that my stay at The Home was a blessing. I think that everyone there was a guiding, positive light in my life. Even the mean nurse, as all experiences are lessons. They are our own seconds in time.

The Closing Door

Our personal clock ticks and we find ourselves moving forward like the hands of a clock, making new memories. We don't realize it while it's happening, but we are being molded by the motions and the actions that tick like a clock, changing with each moment.

Family can be the most beautiful grouping of souls. It is an opportunity to trust totally and to love unconditionally. A security of knowing that no matter what happens in life, they will be there to share and to care. For me, this bond has never been broken.

It is important to share some of my own family history with you so that you understand some of the moments in time that we shared together as they were part of the "bonding" that I write about.

My parents made a happy home. The inside of our house had a strong sense of security with the love that generated through it, and this was another reason why there was a phenomenal closeness of our hearts. I can honestly say that I do indeed feel blessed, as I know no other family as ours. We are all still living, but without the bonding mother whom we all adored. She was the nucleus, the center of the strength, and the aura that we all wanted to step into. She passed away many years ago, and still the power of her words are heard with the loudness of any church bell ringing through the holiday season.

Decisions are still made with her in mind. It is amazing that she managed to affect so many for so long. So phenomenal was this lady that references are continually made to how she would react or how she would feel. How is this possible? I only wish that I had one-third of the "life power" that she had. I continue to try.

Prolonged time in hospitals and time spent around sick people can teach a person to be strong. It can also have a way of changing how a person feels about his or her own sickness, as there always seem to be others who are much sicker; it almost makes you ashamed of feeling sorry for yourself. When you think about it, the mind is a big factor in the healing process. Negativity can break down the attitude, and the stress that results only works against the healing time.

Time traveled in a negative mindset makes the travel more difficult, not only for patients, but for the people who care for them. Most of the time, controlling the mind is not difficult. It is a decision that we can make no matter what the challenge is. I have found through my own experiences that I can find good in most of the "bad." I have found that all of my life lessons have widened my understanding. It can be rough going, but there always seem to be venues of new beginnings along the way that I find are a great contributors to my healing.

Family is so important. It is a natural bond of oneness. I have been blessed with mine, and it is amazing when I think about how these beautiful, wonderful people influenced my life. They are all the reason for my endless faith in life and hope. I cannot explain exactly how I feel, but I know that God was blessing me in other ways by surrounding me with people who cared. He gave me a family that would make sure I stayed strong. I knew I was loved, and they helped me believe I would get better. I was lucky.

There wasn't one person in my family who was better than the others. They all held different levels in different areas of life that made them all equal and all gifted. We had faith in each other, and we had faith in life and love and the knowledge that if we work hard and continue to keep positive attitudes, life's doors to success and happiness will open for us.

The lessons I learned differed from those that my siblings learned. My mother must have had a plan in place in order for all of us to believe in ourselves. It is sad that I missed that year of growing up with my brothers and sisters, but I know that her efforts to keep us all focused worked. Certainly, I did not realize this while I was strapped in traction, but I do now. My own type of molding was taking place.

All of the lessons were the building of "character marks." My mother's interaction with me while I was in The Home that long year taught me sensitivity and trust. I believe that all types of interactions and experiences shared with family are moments that contribute to our growth. From our mother's first touch to the sound of her voice to sharing time reading books, these types of experiences groom us to be who we are. They all count!

It seems as though this beginning was a push toward the path of healing. I was learning mine. I knew my weaknesses and I was starting to realize my strengths. Each of us has our own strengths and weaknesses, and we all manage to find them in our own time. I was simply forced to find mine early in life. When I think about the path I had to follow, I can understand why I think and feel the way I do. I seem to try to be the Band-Aid for everyone at all times. That was my place in the family. I didn't have it alone though, as it was shared among all of us "spirit gardeners"!

My family was lucky at love within. We were however, very unlucky when it came to physical trauma. Obviously, with six children, the chances of experiencing traumas would increase significantly, but I'll bet our family count would have won a prize anyway. It was ridiculous. It is interesting to see how the age position in the family affects the character building with family life.

Research tells us that the firstborn child usually will fit all of the characteristics of just that. For my oldest brother, this was true. He was the first, and he often was the one in charge. This man is very strong and has always carried all of us with him. His broad shoulders were always strong enough to handle it all. He has had his own traumas throughout life but has always managed to stand tall and succeed. His "first" position could be categorized as one of his traumas because, in that role, he managed all of ours. He has a strong look, but a soft heart. No matter what, he would always step in and help us. He has been our guide and our problem solver. I love and admire him very much. He married one of the most wonderful women in the world and they are a perfect match! She has been a *true gift* to our family, and I love her dearly.

My brother carried all of the traditions and the life rules that our parents taught us to his family. I love his children as if they are my own. They are the perfect mix of both of their parents. They are both strong and have great souls, and they mean the world to me. We have a true family connection. My niece now has a daughter who indeed will make a difference in this world. She has the mixture of strength from all of them, and that will be her own secret power.

My second-oldest brother has broad shoulders too. He is one of the most genuine people I know. He has had his share of traumas as well, but his heart of gold still shines brightly. When he enters a room, all eyes seem to turn toward him, and he is indeed very distinguished. He is a leader in his own right, and he is the type of person who would do anything for anybody. He gave his life to his family and deserves all of the respect that anyone could ever give him. He possesses all of the genuine qualities of a great person and I love him deeply! This gentle soul is a gift to all of us. He has two wonderful children and a granddaughter too. Multiple doors have been opening for all. This second brother is with a great woman now, and we all think the match is perfect for him and indeed another blessing.

When my oldest sister was a child, she managed to fall backward out of our kitchen window, tumbling over just in time to land on the handlebars of a bicycle that someone didn't put away. It didn't have the rubber handle cover, and that saved her life. She landed face first, the circular handle puncturing through her clavicle area and saving her from landing on the cement. I believe God saved her so she could continue to do his work, as she is the most Christian of us all. When you hear her voice, you know that she is with you. I don't believe that there are many people in the world who give 100 percent of themselves at all costs, but my sister does. She is a lover of life, and she radiates all the good that life has to offer. She is an angel indeed and always there. Even though it has been from a distance for years, it has never been far. She is a special star put on this earth for all of us to enjoy. A true bright light that we should follow!

My youngest brother experienced an almost deadly drink when he got into his eye medicine and drank it when he was a toddler. I know that my mother must have had fear in her eyes with this trauma because it could have been fatal. Immediate first aid was given, but the rush to the hospital for help was needed. She could

The Closing Door

have easily stabilized a broken bone if that had been the case, but this accident was different. She knew that she had to get him to the hospital quickly. He was, by testing, the most genius level. He is an artist for life and a great soul. He is a deep thinker guided by an inner light. He is the type of person you wouldn't see for years but when you met again, the time seemed short. He has an inner voice that guides him, and with this gift of "spirit strength" he lights the hearts of those who are in his circle. He is a gentle man with many stars to follow, and he has caught many of them. He is gifted in the world of art and in his. He has a wonderful wife and they have been blessed as parents and grandparents. The circle of life continues!

It is strange that my baby sister's trauma was shared with only me. As young adults, we were skiing on a nearby small slope with our older brothers. They happened to take a break and went in for something to eat. We said that we were going to keep skiing for a while and that we would be in later. I always looked for safety first, an immediate outlook and prevention step that has carried me through my professional life to this day. I told her numerous times to stick her long brown hair inside her coat because the rope tow might grab onto it. She didn't listen. Oh God, she didn't listen! It happened so quickly almost seconds after the warning came out of my mouth for the second time. Quickly and amazingly, like a monster, this thick rope took the end of her hair and wrapped it up all of the way to her scalp, lifting her off her feet and carrying her up the hill toward the sharp metal motor.

I screamed as I have never screamed before. I was trapped like in traction, stuck in a moment of helplessness for this little girl whom I loved. I couldn't get my skis off. *I couldn't run — again!* I kept screaming for someone to help, as we were the only ones on the hill. Finally, I got my skis off and began running up the hill, too short to jump up and grab the rope to stop it from taking my sister. I never ran as slowly as it seemed in my mind. All of these moments are so vivid.

Out of nowhere came a man in the dark. He jumped up the pole that didn't have any bolts for footing, and he shimmied up the pole like an outdoor animal. Her face was a foot from the monster's spokes. The churning metal was ready to split her face in half, and she screamed as she saw it coming even closer toward her. Closer... OH MY GOD!

He stuck his foot in the motor, stopping it. He yelled to me how to shut the motor off in a control panel and then pulled my sister down and unwrapped her hair. My brothers were there then. Their faces were in shock, as who would ever think that something like this would happen? We always went skiing, and it was atypical that older brothers would offer to take their younger sisters with them for the evening. They loved us and their painful eyes haunt me to this day. She had a large circle of hair missing from her head. She recovered, of course, and it seems to have affected her less than it affected me. This man out of nowhere just disappeared. I never even got to thank him. It was one of the first "miracles" that I experienced. As it turned out, he worked for the phone company and happened to have his steel boots on. But I still wonder exactly who he was. My sister is now married to a man who builds for a living. He doesn't wear those steel boots, but she knows that he too came to her for a reason. They share time skiing on mountains that are higher than the one that almost killed her, and they have been building ever since. Together they have conquered many obstacles and are more successful than most. I love to visit with them, and they continue to stay deeply connected to all of us. She has a great love for family, and she continues to make a difference in all of our lives.

These are only a few of the traumas that we went through as a family, but we managed to make it through them all. Mother didn't work as a nurse while we were all little. She had all of her training put to use at home the entire time we were growing up. She was a true master of time!

Since time always played a major part of my thought processing, the time that I spent thinking and waiting seemed to be a silent playground for me. It was an escape and a place filled with only my thoughts and my conclusions.

The Closing Door

The months passed after I returned from The Home, and I adjusted to my new life in my real home. I would wake up and my mother would be there to say good morning. Then she would put my brace on my leg. It must have been funny to see me in my nightgown with high-topped brown shoes. I still didn't feel different even though I walked with a brace and crutches, but my method of making the days pass quickly seemed to become harder to do. I wanted to be free from the structures that were holding me up. The constant love from my mother was a support that not only made my healing easier but managed to make me feel like I wasn't different at all.

As I mentioned, I never thought that my siblings might feel like I got too much attention. We all felt equally loved, and my mother used to treat us that way. She was very attentive to each one of us and, therefore, there wasn't any jealousy or hard feelings about where the attention was going. There were so many of us that there wasn't time to concentrate on just one person. We all blended together. I may have turned out differently if that weren't the case. There are many factors that melded into one, and I am just grateful that my challenge didn't create any additional problems.

Who we are is a result of our experiences and environment. Some people never witness traumatic events that necessitate major thoughts on the subject. It is strange when I think of that! I believe that we all gained strength from the challenge. My trauma offered my family members another reason to knit our souls into one. They tell me now that they just missed me and were glad that I was home. I don't think that any of them can imagine how much I missed each one of them.

Obviously, my recovery meant special attention from my mother that the others didn't get. But much of it was far from fun! Three times a day, my mother lifted me onto the dining room table to go through a series of exercises, lifting weights that were connected to my ugly brown shoe. It was very difficult to lift my foot up so that my knee was straight. Painful too!

The hinge continued to get stuck on my skin, and we never figured out how to stop that from happening. I remember having to stay in and exercise my leg while everyone else was out playing. It was monotonous, and I hated that.

My parents didn't shelter me, though, and I went out to play with my brothers and sisters as well as the other children in our neighborhood. I know I used to feel like I could keep up and run like the wind, even with those crutches at my sides. Funny, I always used to run quickly down the very same hill that was my last hill climb before I ended up in the D.T. Watson Home. Maybe subconsciously I wanted to conquer that hill!

Five years later, I was permitted to stop wearing my brace. I remember being disappointed that I still had to wear orthopedic shoes but happy that my ugly brace would be gone! It was as if I faltered again, losing my ability to master my attitude. There was a little corner store in the heart of Sewickley that my mother used to take me to for shoes. They were not in style yet either, but they did give me the support I needed.

I learned all the tricks one can learn if given enough time to adjust. I remember the day my grandmother told me to open the corner cabinet in her buffet because there was something inside of it just for me. I limped over and opened the cabinet slowly in anticipation and certainly not like a child that cannot wait to see. I wanted to savor the moment. I gasped as I saw a shiny pair of black, patent leather Mary-Janes. I cried then, and I cry as I write this. That moment was another one that changed me. I sat on my grandmother's soft, comfortable lap and kissed her cheeks over and over again. My shoes! Mine! I could wear them only on special occasions, but it was my time now!

Time...it is fragile. I have spoken of many but I have to tell you about a man who has always been there for me and a man whom I cherish. It is my father. He too stood by my bedside in the D.T. Watson Home, and he stood by my mother's side as well. He stood by all of us, this tall man with silver hair. He is very distinguished looking and a powerful strength within me. Just like the night that I was afraid of Santa finding only me when he came down our chimney. My mother slept beside me that night, but I still knew that my father would be a different kind of protector. His daily phone calls are a reminder that he is still here for me today. He and my mother were my special seconds in time. They gave me the love I needed and filled my days with sunshine. I love them both.

The experiences we have are seconds in time, but the memories last forever. All of these "seconds" build into a lifetime. They are mirror images of which we are all one. It was a small family cosmos to the universal cosmos. We are significant and insignificant all at the same time. Having my family there to walk with me filled my seconds with security. We would walk together through time.

Our mother was the one who stayed home and was the life teacher. Time was limited, as there were many to manage. She always placed written messages on the refrigerator and around the house for us to read. A way of managing her time, I guess. By doing this, she was assured that she was doing all she could for us to gain knowledge and expand our worlds. From our individual vocabulary lists to large life lessons.

The following is just a tiny example of the type of "lessons" that she would post for us to read and to think about. Like the Irish blessing, this Old English prayer known as "Take Time" is often varied in its interpretation, and the author is not known. My mother posted this for us as noted below:

"Seconds in Time"
Take time to work – it is the price of success.
Take time to think – it is the source of power.
Take time to play – it is the secret of perpetual youth.
Take time to read – it is the fountain of wisdom.
Take time to be friendly – it is the road to happiness.
Take time to dream – it is hitching your wagon to a star.
Take time to love and be loved – it is the privilege of the God.
Take time to look around – it is too short of a day to be selfish.
Take time to laugh – it is the music of the soul.

Dee Van Balen

This poem ended up in her personal journal, for she valued how perfectly it stated the important things we should concentrate on in life. Statements that would make our "seconds in time" more meaningful. She knew we would read them. She knew, this Master of Life, that she would always try hard to be the best mother in the world. She succeeded in her goal of giving us great roots and the messages of the true meaning of life and love. She helped us to move forward with the strength of many.

CHAPTER 5
BELIEVING IN MAGIC

CHAPTER FIVE:
Believing in Magic

I have always believed in magic! Not the human performance that tricks the eyes, but in the magic of life. There exists here on earth magical situations that are almost too hard to believe. Like the birds that used to be my personal clock outside the window of my hospital room in The Home. It was my own magic of managing! It may have been a small, insignificant magic to someone else, but it was my magic just the same.

There is magic in love and there is magic in the ability to believe! The Home high on the hill…I believed and my wish came true. I was in control! It was my mind's magical ability to believe and that is just a part of what helped me get through it. It is true, all of the thoughts of many that we have to be positive to manage. We have to be able to see, as they say, the glass half full. Our attitudes enable us to manage. Yes…all of the people that surround us with love and affection keep us on that magical path of belief.

Many different holidays throughout the year are intertwined with "magic" for children. Christmas is the holiday for all to believe in magic or the spirit of Christmas.

A helping hand to another, a small gesture of friendship, and small gifts for caring…all of this magic seeps into the soul of those who took time to make a difference. And isn't it true that when people try to help others they end up helping themselves? No matter what, being kind to others always makes you feel better about yourself.

Christmas…the perfect holiday. It is a time when joy is in the air and decorations state that it is the season for love and giving. It is the most memorable holiday season of all for me. As children, we used to look forward to the day when we took my father's company truck to go to the farm and cut down our Christmas tree. We all rode on the wagon and picked it together. Hot chocolate and Mancini's toast was waiting for us on our return.

The Closing Door

My brothers put the tree up but only Santa decorated it on Christmas Eve! So when we woke up, we gathered on the steps that led from the bedrooms and sang "Happy Birthday" to Jesus. This was a tradition in our family and one that I admire my parents for, as it kept the meaning of the holiday in perspective! Yes...it was the birthday of Jesus.

After the song, we would all start to scream and run down the steps and into the living room. The lights on the tree would be shining brilliantly with ornaments and tinsel, and the lights around it were grand! I think that this vision was one of the most splendid of the day. I know that it sounds strange, but it was more about seeing that tree than the gifts that were surrounding it.

With the six of us, there were many gifts piled up to be opened. Even if they were not all for me, it looked unbelievable!

We all had an allowance and we saved to buy special gifts for our parents and each other. My father was very hard to buy for, and he always would shake the box and try to figure out what was inside of it. He always seemed to manage to guess.

One Christmas, though, I had bought glass piggy banks for them. This was my shining moment, as he did not figure that one out. He and I shared the joy and laughter of his guess not being correct, and I think that was the longest hug that I have ever received from him! It wasn't about the amount of money that I'd spent, it was about the thought that had gone into my present.

I liked sports, not dolls. Dolls bored me. After all, I had spent a lot of time in bed high up on that hill, so sitting down and playing with dolls was not how I wanted to spend my free time. I wanted to play and run all day if I could! But my choice in gifts was mostly jewelry. I loved rings. It seemed like I could keep these things forever. I preferred a lasting gift from my parents. These gifts would last forever and remind me of the magic of love and the strength that we receive from loved ones.

Christmas is the season to believe! The spirit of the season is magnificent!

I experienced another miracle moment the year that our daughters informed us of the true gifts that they wanted Santa to bring them — after we had already purchased their presents. Money was tight that year, and we were frugal with our purchases. But visualizing the smiles on our daughters' faces was all that really mattered. So my mother and I ran out to a toy store to find a talking doll and a red guitar and microphone. It was only a few days until Christmas, and who would have thought that success would even be a possibility?

Much to our surprise, we found the talking doll. Someone had just returned it! I looked at the price tag and shuddered. My personal ability to believe was starting to shatter, but I put it in the cart anyway. Then around the corner, just as if it was waiting for us, we saw a stand-up microphone! The picture on the front was so cute, with a little girl playing a guitar and singing into this cool microphone. It too went into the cart.

The line waiting to check out was very long, and I nervously anticipated spending more money. But I told myself it was the season to sacrifice for the happiness of my children. Ironically enough, there was extra cash beside my secret holding area for "emergency" money. I laughed and to this day still wonder if my mom put that "extra cash" in there.

I stayed up late that evening and wrapped the gifts. Our tree was already decorated, as I didn't keep that part of my parents' tradition alive. But the next morning our daughters sat on our steps in their pajamas and sang "Happy Birthday" to Jesus.

They opened their presents and looked so happy. Then I told them Santa had left one more gift for them that they had yet to open. They started jumping up and down with glee, hoping for those special items that were on their lists.

The Closing Door

Our oldest daughter opened hers first, and I will never forget her expression when she pulled out her talking doll. She was just at the age not to believe...but that morning she screamed that now she knew there was a Santa! This event made her wonder for another year or so. When our youngest daughter stood up to open her gift, she pulled out what we were thinking she would...a stand-up microphone. But out of that box she also pulled not a black or brown guitar but a *red guitar* along with that microphone! My husband and I were shocked, and I started to cry. That moment reinvigorated my Christmas spirit and further secured my belief in the magic of Santa!

Whether it is the spirit of Christmas or the personal feeling of love, it is magical. I still believe in magic and the spirit of Christmas. I believe in life and I believe there are small miracles every day for us to see. All we have to do is open our eyes and look.

CHAPTER 6
WALKING THROUGH LIFE

CHAPTER SIX:
Walking through Life

My past was the basis, my "Beginning," and my Half Smile was my managing. The "Different Doors" that opened and closed became the life path I would follow and my ability to believe, not just in magic but in myself, became much easier. Walking is easy, but if we want to run, we cannot learn from the moments in time that were there for us to learn from, unless we go over in our minds what we learned from them. They may be redundant at times, in the theories of the "why," but that is because we need the reasons behind those words to learn from the history that preceded them.

When I think back to how I depended on those crutches to keep me up, I know that the people who walked with me when I was younger kept my steps from being wobbly. As I got older, I found myself being disappointed when the people who were supposed to be walking with me were not. Time spent in The Home has given me the fortitude to continue to believe and have faith that people are still good. I feel that even when people stray from what is considered "right," there is reason in their actions because of their own experiences. We are *all* products of our past.

To go back in time and explain how my path unfolded is easy now, and the desire to be active and sensitive to life was as well. The drive to understand motion and feel the connection between people was easy too. It was fascinating to me. I enjoyed joining all the sport teams that I could, and I trusted in the hearts of many along the way. The impact of my experience drove me into my future, and my years of trauma and loss made me not even realize it as I stepped forward smiling. After years of happiness mixed with challenges throughout my life, it was time that I put my puzzle together. I got it, as they say. I will also share the fact that the development of my limbs may have taken many years, but the lasting effect of the time capsule of healing brought multiple aspects both good and bad to my life.

The Closing Door

This was how I developed a trust in all people and a trust in the inherent goodness of their actions. I believe in their words as well, and this is another reason why I look at life the way I do. I carried all that I had experienced with me into a wide world of others. Open eyes and blinded eyes at the same time.

The memory of the leaves dancing with the wind at The Home still moves me. Motion was music to me back then, and understanding what made those leaves move was like magic. I loved, and still love, to analyze motion. Learning how and why the body moves was an interest that I understood when I studied it. One movement affects another, and one muscle causes one motion as it causes the opposite action in another. Just like when I was strapped in traction at The Home, I could feel the motion just thinking about it. It was always as if I were moving too. Gymnastics, dance, and diving were my favorite types of movement. I felt the "dance" of it all. I felt the rhythm, and the moves were music to my soul. I could feel each hesitation between notes and the exhilaration of the next beat. It was expression from the gut! My body couldn't move back then, but my mind could follow.

It enabled me to release my pain by stepping with the timing of it all in my mind, and with fire in my heart. Back then, the leaves seemed to be telling me a silent story of the beauty of motion and guiding me to it. I could follow the leaves' movements, swaying with the wind. They were still for a moment and then they picked up speed and flipped over and over again with the force of the wind beneath them. It was my own movie of sorts, passing time away. So I had made a path of healing through thoughts. I entertained myself watching life passing, connecting things around me in my mind as my story was developing. I treasured nature from a distance. I touched it with my mind through my tiny window. I believed in life, and I believed in people. They were all walking with me smiling. This would be my path and my expression of self.

Approximately five years or so after I was first diagnosed with polio, I didn't need my crutches anymore. I sat in my backyard, very close to the place where my mother noticed that I was limping, and a breeze blew against my face. It was a windy day, and the breeze that blew against my face was certainly not like the touch of it from inside of my room at The Home. At that moment, I could feel the breeze lift me. I reached out, picked up the most beautiful orange leaf, and stared at it. Laughing I made it spin with my fingers. The crutches were gone. I was free at last.

Time still followed the same path, only now I was safe in my own bed. My alarm would no longer be a nurse waking me up. I would be able to walk into the kitchen and have breakfast with my wonderful family. I knew that I was strong but still sensitive in the areas of the heart. Part of the "Haunting," I guess.

I still never stopped to think all the way through high school and my university years about why I was so sensitive to life. I seemed to be able to look at traumas as just that, but if someone would hit my heart with words or actions, my response was not good. I had trained myself to address personal challenges, and I managed to find a way through them. I just couldn't find a way to filter pain of the heart. These types of situations to this day are not ones that I respond to very well. I trust and I believe and that is it! Even when I am misunderstood, always feel strongly that person I admire should also admire me and know that I meant no harm. I had experienced too much trauma as a young child ever to want to do that! Interactions and loves came and made their mark. I was growing older and coming closer to the age where now I could be one of the people that could help others. I could now have a chance to step in and maybe make a difference in someone's life. Now it was my turn and I walked with the music that was in my soul ready to face life's next step.

Friends were plentiful and life was grand, and life continued to follow the path of time. I was healthy and anxious to greet each new day. I dated many but always stayed true to myself and the honor that my family had instilled in all of us. Our home was still home and we were always welcome there. The number of people sitting around the table grew and so did the happiness.

I had a great childhood and a phenomenal family life so I thought that life was just like that! I was certain I would marry the man of my dreams and continue the path that I had been exposed to as a child. After all, I was a believer! I trusted in myself and in life. Why not?

All of the men I had dated were wonderful. Each one still has a special place in my heart. We were friends and spent time walking through life. We built memories together that are lasting. I admire them to this day. Life pulled us apart and new steps took each of us onto other paths.

My mother dropped me off at the university, and I suddenly found myself adopting a quiet personality. I didn't realize it then, but now I know that it was a piece of the puzzle left over from my past connecting my future to The Home. I just felt out of place not being with my family, and I certainly did not cherish the feeling of being alone. I had had enough of that when I was little. I was farther away than I had ever been before, and I guess the thoughts were frightening. My silence continued, but not for long. My power from The Home soon took over, and the walk was easy. I was homesick, yes, but definitely not shy.

I was adventurous and traveled throughout Europe as a young university student. I made sure that I had all of the experiences that I could have to expose me to life and love. Since I had the experience in The Home when I was young my view on life and what it had to offer was unlimited so I took advantage of it.

I traveled by myself and met many people that managed to influence my life as a result of it. I remember being on a train traveling to Holland and I didn't know exactly which train to transfer to. Without the language expertise, it was somewhat difficult. There was an older woman on the train and she smiled at me but hesitated to speak. I was afraid of being in the wrong area and wanted only to have someone tell me which train to take for my desired destination.

When we finally stopped, she gave me flowers and told me, in English, which way to go. I was grateful at the time and certainly happy to have someone finally help me and I hugged her goodbye. Later

I was disturbed as to why she didn't help me earlier. Interesting…I still believed, and maybe shouldn't have.

I was lucky enough to have a great roommate who shared the next four years with me. We had fun stepping through time together and learned many other lessons in life. Having a friend that I could trust with me was fun. Eventually we lost touch with each other, as our paths changed, but we recently found one another again and our life path connected again.

One very special person, my best friend outside of my family, is to this day my best friend and sister. I will refer to her as Mae. She graduated before me, and we lost touch too. One day while I was still in school, my boyfriend mentioned that there was a girl teaching in my old high school who said that she knew me. It was Mae! Shocked at this news, I drove home the next weekend, and our magical friendship began again.

Mae married one of my best friends from high school. They were a perfect match and a magical pair. They have two children whom I adore, and they are like my own family. They are another connection. One is my true godchild, and the other is too, though not on paper. They both are wonderful. This "silent godchild" has been my little secret "life giver" during these years of her adulthood. She has a heart of gold. The seconds in time with all of them have been marks of my life that I treasure.

My mother used to always say that if you have one really true friend when you are older that you should consider yourself very lucky. I never really understood that then, but I do now! She is the friend that doesn't walk beside you during troubled times. She is the one that walks with you!

Like the verse about the footsteps in the sand. A photo of only one person walking but there is another set of footprints in stride right beside you. Those footprints are God, as the verse goes, and it is a verse that I know is correct. Well, her footsteps are a life force within me, stepping forward together like no other. She is a guide for me, other than my family and a person that must have been

The Closing Door

my sister in another life, if there is such a thing. She is indeed my sister now.

I realize that a special friend is a gift. It is an unconditional bond that nothing can break. It is a magical force of hearts that beat as one. There isn't anything that I wouldn't do for this friend. We share our troubles and secrets of life. We share conversations that are healing, analyzing the whys of the world and why people are the way they are. We complain about what is bothering us when we know that we don't have anyone else to tell. We know that we can't share many topics with family members because they will worry unnecessarily. We share so they don't have to worry and therefore we keep them from stress. I have never had a situation that she couldn't help me through. She has a questioning method of madness that makes you say what is on your mind and helps you see all sides of a situation. She is the great rule reader. She is the guru of quotes and clichés. She is my buddy and my calm.

I met the man that I would marry. I walked into a holiday gathering and walked out with a new beginning. It all started with a gentle tap upon my shoulder. It was my dear friend I had grown up with. His name was RD. He is a happy soul, and has always reminded me of my oldest brother. He too has strong shoulders and a gift of conversation that would bring calm to any challenging time. He is a man that I will always consider to be a brother. He has walked through most of my life with me, and has been a positive force at all times. I trust him! He is a true friend, and one that will always be my "crutch." He is the mixture of my real family with his caring ways, and he has all of the heart that matches my "family" at The Home. He is my stabilizer and my extension of love. My family is growing.

RD introduced me to my future husband, without those words of course, and the man he introduced me to I had already known for years. I knew his family, so he was not a stranger by any means. He asked me to dance, and I said yes. He took my hand softly and led me to the dance floor. It was a slow song, and he moved like the rhythm of the wind. A gentle glide into a sequence of rhythms that felt perfect. We were a match! We were in tune with the music and each other. Dancing with him was like the magic of the "dance of the leaves" and my heart pounded rapidly just thinking about it. My pulse was rapid too, and I didn't understand this feeling I was experiencing.

He literally swept me off my feet. He held me close, and his hands were strong. We didn't dance long, but we didn't need to. The union was made, and I cannot explain this. It just happened.

We rejoined the group but not really. Our eyes were drawn to each other, and it was intense. I had driven to this dance with other friends from high school, and I had never left any place with anyone other than those I had gone with. It was a personal rule. But this time the rule would be broken. I felt safe, and so it was done, and we left. We laughed all the way home, and I had so much fun. We drove up to my house, and he walked me to my door. I opened the door and he stepped inside. I said good night and thank you.

At that moment, as I stood on the step making me taller than I was, he reached up and put his warm hands on my cheeks and leaned in to kiss me gently on the lips. Then he just looked into my eyes and I melted. Silence...

He was a gentle man and one that I fell deeply in love with. I thought that we were a perfect match, and our time together was exactly as I had envisioned it to be my whole life. Another addition to our family who was a perfect fit. I expected to have the fairy tale come true, and it did.

I was the princess and he was my knight in shining armor. It was a glorious time. Our lives melted easily together as one. We traveled distances, while we were apart, just to be with one another, and the moments that we shared were treasured. His hug was strong and comforting. I felt the power of love within me just as I did up high on that hill when I was young, only my door wasn't closing.

We stepped together into the future by choice, holding hands every step of the way. We laughed often and a natural molding of our hearts evolved. I used to laugh because when he walked into a room and I saw him, my heart skipped a beat and I gasped for a moment. I thought it was a silent response, but people around us saw this reaction and they teased me about it.

On a magic mountain, he put his hands on my face and said that he loved me. He held me in his arms and he asked me if I would marry him and have his children. We kissed as we had never kissed before and whispered those three magical words, "I love you." The night was dark, but the stars in the sky were plentiful. They twinkled in the sky and it seemed as though they were celebrating, clapping with the beat of our hearts.

My wedding dress was perfect. It was elegant and feminine. The lace flowed from the mid-forearm down to my hands and had beautiful lace entwined through the end with a small, delicate bow. It had a fitted waist and a long train. My floppy lace hat matched perfectly, and the lace from the back of it was almost as long as the train on my gown. I loved it. And he was so handsome! Yes, I was walking through time.

Time...it was always something that I didn't take for granted. I had learned how to manipulate it in The Home. I made it work for me. Now the beats of my heart were ticking with time, and I moved with each second without any need to try to adjust it. Many doors had closed and opened in my life, and I felt ready to enter this new door with a man that I loved. We were married on a sunny day. I received a dozen red roses from him in the early morning before our wedding. The card read, "See you at noon." That was the time we were set to say our vows.

The roses were a perfect touch of romance that calmed the anticipation of the day, and a true expression of love that I will never forget. I still have the card.

But I was very nervous about walking down that aisle. Many people were getting separated and divorced and even though I felt confident, I was still nervous.

It seemed like hours waiting for my moment to walk down the aisle! Finally, the music began to play and my walk toward my future began. My handsome, wonderful father had my arm, and I felt safe, just as he had made me feel all of my life. Just like the night that I felt his presence when I was allowed to be transported home to spend just one night at home on Christmas Eve when I was little. I was afraid that Santa would come down that chimney and see only me. It was scary. He protected me from the fear of seeing Santa alone back then and now my protector was leading me down the aisle to a man that would be my own shining knight and my Santa for the rest of my life. He trusted this man that would soon be mine and he placed my hand into his with confidence.

My faith in God is deep, and I talk to him in private, just as I would a friend. I trust in the fact that he listens to me. During the ceremony, I looked up at the engrained sculpture of our Lord and silently asked him to make sure that our marriage would last forever. When I made that sacred bond, it was forever.

There is a song called "Time in a Bottle" by Jim Croce that we wanted to have played in our wedding. I had spent many years focusing on "time" while I was living on the Hill, and this was a song that told my story. It was about living your life with someone you loved and longed to be with forever.

All of my dreams and beliefs in life were wrapped up in that song. It was a love story and one that I felt in the depths of my soul. It was a magnificent wedding and reception. We were the last to leave! I wasn't going to follow tradition and be picked up and carried out of our reception. I could dance and I could *walk* so we stayed and celebrated with everyone the entire night! I had come a long way since that child's hospital bed in the D.T. Watson Home.

We left for our honeymoon, and I knew that even though another door was closing behind me, this new door was shining brightly. We walked forward, hand-in-hand, with our own light radiating each second together. We had our own magic, and the man who stood beside me was the love of my life. We would grow old together, as we promised each other. I felt so blessed, and now my magic was twofold. We headed south for the celebration, and the sun that shined upon us couldn't match the love-light in our hearts. We were blessed.

Like a revolving door, soon our celebration time ended and we were back at home again before we knew it. The excitement of the trip was still fresh in our minds, and the sun-kissed color on our skin was another sign that we had made a start to our new beginning. The feeling I had that first night together when he held me would be a feeling that would stay strong in my heart and in my soul forever. His gentle kiss was mine, and mine was his.

We arranged to continue our education out west. We quit our teaching positions in Pennsylvania, packed up all of belongings, and headed out for our journey into our future. It was a difficult step for both of us to leave our loved ones and friends behind, but we were ready to greet our new adventure. We traveled far west into a new life and arrived without harm, entering our new space in life as one.

Our long travel to this new destination was an exciting trip. We were alone for a long while, and the newness of it all was thrilling. It is strange how different the land is between states. There were not many trees in this new land, and it felt odd. It did possess a unique beauty of its own though, with flowing wheat fields and beautiful blue sky hovering over us like a massive blanket. It was amazing. It surrounded us. I could put my hand out to my sides, just below my waistline, and turn a circle that would outline the skyline.

Just like any change in life, this new place was different. We drove up to our new home, and the wind was powerful. My long hair was unruly, and the wind picked it up and swirled it around like a movie. Our first few days were strange, as we didn't know anyone. But soon we found the people of the "flatland" to be very kind. Our adjustment didn't take long, and we were happy in this new place. We were far away from home, but together.

We were both going to be graduate students, and I was not sure of how I felt about it. I had already graduated from my university and had a position teaching. To leave that and once again enter school seemed odd and made me feel out of place. Typically, after you are in a new environment for a little while it starts to feel comfortable. The fact that I was nervous at first was normal. We all have a hard time with the anticipation of starting something new. This anticipation can cause confidence levels to drop, and time is wasted in the state of being unsure of oneself. I was a master of the "unknown," referring to all the times when I was little being certain that I would hear the words, "You are healed." But it wasn't working for me now. I couldn't erase the nervousness I was experiencing. This period of uncertainty didn't last long, as my secret power to believe kicked in and erased the nervousness. Besides…I had my knight with me.

This adjustment is a result of my start on the Hill. It gave me a different insight on life. Sometimes it didn't work immediately, but I always managed eventually to find the calm within me. I knew I had the confidence to face these new challenges with my "learned inner strength."

I was drawn by a desire to help others, and my choice to be a teacher came naturally. I wanted to see the excitement in my students' faces when they addressed a challenge and found answers. I was thrilled to see them be proud of themselves because of their success, and this filled my heart with joy and drove me to work even harder. To be able to have a job that enables you to be even a small part in someone's raised confidence level is a blessing. I loved this part of teaching, and it was a part of my field that I focused on. Believing! I loved to set the stage for all of them to believe in themselves and to develop their self-concepts. I didn't want them to put limits on their goals for their futures. Sometimes their faces would remind me of my little friends in The Home. The sparkle in their eyes let me know that they too believed.

I believed. Why not? I walked without a limp! Anything was possible.

CHAPTER 7
THE ICY NIGHT

CHAPTER SEVEN:
The Icy Night

It was late in the evening and I was busy typing a thesis for my master's program. My husband's co-worker came into our home, and our travel began. I didn't want to go, as I had far too much work ahead of me. But I went anyway. This would have been the perfect time for me to listen to the inner voice telling me not to go and to abide by the suggestion. I did not pay attention!

They told us that two different cars hit us. I don't remember anything. I have tried for years but it won't come back. I don't really want to remember, but it feels odd that I have no recollection of parts of this traumatic event. The stories that the medical personnel told us about that horrible icy night are our only means of knowledge. I usually was the one who erased bad feelings as if they never occurred, just like when I had to leave my home on Christmas Day to go back to The Home as a little girl. This time God helped me to erase this tragic time.

I believe that it was His way of protecting me. I remember the first part of our drive and the moment that I woke up for about a minute to find that I was in a hospital bed once again. A few weeks later, when I could finally be taken off the medication that kept me in the "coma state of mind," I woke up just to find myself in another nightmare!

Going back in time, I remember sitting in the back seat with luggage around me. But that was about an hour before the accident. My legs were crossed like a pretzel, and I was leaning forward with my elbows on the back of the front seat chatting away. It was dark. Only six years later did I remember out of the blue saying, "Oh no…Where is the road?" The roads where we lived were all straight, running north-to-south and east-to-west. Bending in the road was not a typical terrain, and it was this bend that stopped time for all of us. A violent accident that ended in such tragedy! The man traveling toward us crossed the center line and hit the back of our

The Closing Door

car, putting us into a spin, and we slid sideways forward, and the oncoming second car smashed right into us. I wish I could go back and alter that second in time.

We lost our dear friend in that tragedy, and to this day, I can hardly think about that. He was a sweet man with children and a wife, and that moment changed all our lives forever! We continue to this day to pray for him and his family. It wasn't our fault, but the pain has still crippled us.

The suitcases slammed my body from head to toe like a twisting tornado to the point that I was unrecognizable. My head swelled up, and every limb of my body was affected by the impact. The medical staff informed us that while they were trying to cut me out of the car my husband kept taking off the straps that held him to the stretcher and walking the fields calling for me. I was yelling for him too while they were trying to cut me out of the car, but neither of us knew this of course. They told us that we were also having normal conversations with them, but they knew that we did not have any idea what we were saying or what was happening to us. The trauma was too severe. When I think about how dramatic the moments were that followed the second impact, I shudder. It still scares me to this day.

They got us to the closest hospital and stage two of our nightmare began. My husband was admitted, as he had lost much blood. The doctors immediately put me in an induced "coma state" so that I wouldn't be able to move and cause any more damage. The ambulance personnel transported me in the position that they found me in because they were worried that if they straightened my legs it would cut my artery and I would bleed to death. My head and entire body had swelled so much that I looked like I weighed three hundred pounds.

My face was black and blue just like my body, and my light blonde hair looked pink from the blood and shiny glass that covered it. The glass and dried blood stayed a part of me for weeks because it couldn't be removed. Any movement of my head or body could have been life threatening. Like Snow White asleep in bed, I was totally unaware of what had happened and what was happening to me. Unlike Snow White, I woke up to another traumatic event.

It was a small hospital filled with brilliant smiles and gentle souls. It was a time in space that I wasn't aware of until I woke up weeks later. My traction was on the leg opposite the one where it had been in The Home. There was a pin through my knee for stabilization. It was a large pin that had loops on the sides for attaching. I was an adult now, but once again unable to walk.

Flat on my back, I had the same view of myself as I'd had in The Home. This time, I couldn't move any part of my body, and I felt isolated from life, confused, and in so much pain. I was old enough to realize the severity of it all, and my gift of tricking time wasn't working.

It was weeks before I opened my eyes for the first time, and they happened to be looking immediately at the doorway to my hospital room. This time the door was open. As my eyelids lifted so did my spirit: there was my sweet mother's face smiling at me again. I sighed with relief and knew that everything would now be OK. My strength had arrived.

My mother would once again have to take care of me. Oddly enough, I awakened for only that brief minute just as my mother had arrived and was standing in my hospital room doorway. I passed out again right after I told her that I loved her, and I didn't awaken again for about a week. When I did, there she was, my beautiful mother sitting by my side and gazing at me with her healing face of hope. We were in a different state, but a very familiar space.

My husband was in the hospital for approximately two weeks. He had trauma to his chest and lost a lot of blood. The doctors kept him very still and within this time his body healed. He was deeply affected by the trauma that occurred that icy night, and even though it wasn't his fault, the emotional pain of the event was overwhelming. The pain from the horrific event was life changing.

The Closing Door

He had to return to the town where we had left that deadly night, and I found myself alone again. The nights were darker than the sky's color, and my mind raced with disbelief from all that had happened. Not only didn't I believe what had happened, but I couldn't believe I was in traction again! The tears that slowly ran down my cheeks were silent streams that I kept from view. My husband and I talked on the phone a few times a day, and when I heard his voice, I felt calm. One night I wasn't very calm and I happened to be talking with my youngest brother. He felt the strain in my voice. There was silence for a moment and then he made one of the most profound statements that I have ever heard. He said, "Just close your eyes and exhale through your smile." I have never forgotten those positive words, and I still use that method of managing when life challenges arise.

The time passed, just as before, and a different window was my escape and my time blocker. I ended up spending three months in that room, hooked up to traction. The tricks that I used to depend on to change my mood didn't work this time and the sounds that awakened me were unchanging. It certainly was not like the seasons that passed my window up the Hill. The weather during the time that I was in that hospital was mixed, with threats of tornadoes alternating with calm skies. The staff at the hospital promised me that they would protect me by covering my bed with blankets, since the shelter was in the hall and my traction wouldn't fit through the door. I just laughed and said not to worry, that a tornado wouldn't hit us.

But, oh my goodness…it did! The windows in my room open with the blinds down, as the safety instructions read. Hail as big as golf balls was bouncing around on my hospital room floor. The wind whirled around and the frightening feeling of being sucked into a tornado was now facing me!

Sirens roared, making my skin crawl. I just couldn't believe it was happening, and I kept saying, "Are you kidding? This is ridiculous!" I stayed positive, though, as once again a caring staff of professionals protected me. Then the phone rang. I answered it, even though it was probably not a great idea as far as safety goes.

It was my husband, and I was so glad to hear his voice! The sound of my husband's voice started the tears rolling down my face, and my positive attitude almost disappeared immediately. I guess the old feeling of being alone instantly entered my mind, and I lost control of my strength. He didn't know that a tornado was hitting the town, and the fright in his voice frightened me as well. In the end, everything was OK.

Soon, it was time for a new step in this new hospital. I was stable and the plan was to put my entire body in a cast for protection and to fly me home to a large hospital where I could have the higher-tech treatment I needed. They rolled me down another hall that I had never seen before and started the process. The body cast was warm and massive. It covered three-quarters of my body. Of course, this new step toward recovery heightened my hope, and the thought of being home was thrilling! Here I go again...

Another door closed, but this time it was behind me. I wasn't walking through a new door, but I was passing through it. I asked the ambulance to stop at a local parish where my friend was a priest so I could say good-bye, and they agreed to do it. My friend and I prayed together, and he promised he would fly to us and visit. What a great man.

Then we continued our journey to the airport, and they walked me up into the plane, stretcher and all, and hooked my stretcher into three first class seats for the ride home. My mother was with me, and she was so cute and excited about our travel home...at last. She had a glass of wine to celebrate, and I could feel her happiness, which was shared with mine. No Half-Smile now. This was real!

My sweet priest friend — whom I had adopted as a relative — was left behind. He was the added strength for us during this time and had the power of calm that is a gift from God. He played cards well and was a great cook. He changed all of our lives and he too is now gone. The people of that small town don't have any idea how powerful this strong man was. He had the heart of a special soul and indeed chose the correct profession. We were lucky to meet him, and

The Closing Door

we gained a family member for life. I always used to think he was placed in that small town for me. I look at his rosary beads, a gift from him, as I type this story. They remind me of him and remind me to be strong. There are so many caring people in this world. It is easy to find them, as many times they come to us without asking. The puzzle of life keeps adding parts, and the picture gets bigger.

The sign was once again placed above the entrance to my home and the same brothers and sisters were there, though much taller this time, as they waited to greet us. "Welcome Home!" The stretcher was replaced by a hospital bed that they had set up in the living room, my new home. Again, the bed was my only environment of "self space." The faces were so kind, and I am certain that major healing of bones was going on as we shared smiles. Of course, this time I wasn't afraid of Santa.

Months passed and my "mind-time-tricking" was practiced. Each trip for a report and new cast was followed by the application of a new mold. My mind was not following the "molding." I went into these appointments positive and never had the report that matched. I know that it is better, at least for me, to be positive and deal with the negative when it comes. Each time that the prognosis was not what I wished to hear, I would continue the learned response of my Half-Smile and go home.

What no one knew, though, was that I used to hide my face and cry with these events. I cried in private so no one would hear. It was a silent place for me to release the emotional pain that I had, and a place where it wouldn't affect anyone else. They wouldn't know, so they wouldn't feel bad. I never wanted anyone to feel bad.

This behavior started when I first awakened that icy night after our car was made to spin out of control. I made sure that no one would see me crashing into tears…*ever*. It was hard to see the pain in others' faces, so it was better to keep smiling. I already felt terrible that people had to take care of me again. I was helpless. Would this ever stop? Remember, that "Half-Smile Molding"?

Finally my husband moved back home, and we lived in the living room of my parents' home. They made it cozy, and we felt comfortable. We would stay for years to come, as I didn't heal for many years. My husband was very sweet throughout this traumatic time. He was such a kind man, and I knew that his heart was breaking thinking about all that had happened. Even though he wasn't at fault for the accident, the pain he carried was heavy. He had lost a friend and almost lost his wife. No one ever found out who first hit us, and I wonder how that person's life has changed. I also wonder where we both would be if this horrific accident had not occurred. I am certain that our professional lives would be much different, but the bond between us would not. Multiple doors had closed and opened throughout my life to this point, and I was determined to make sure that it wouldn't be long until I could walk through one.

Kismet? *Our* fate?

It is said that things happen for a reason. It is also said that even though we don't understand why things happen the way they do, there is a reason behind it. This is exactly what my mother used to say. When I look back now I can understand this, as I have found the positive out of the negative situations that have happened. But I still wonder if part of it was just a way to emotionally find a feeling of calm in a situation when there wasn't any. Is it also a behavior mechanism that fits the situation? Maybe it is also a way for us to gain insight into a situation and therefore enable us to adjust.

Regardless of what helps us get through our own traumas, we change from them and have the opportunity to develop a different outlook or a new understanding of life and living. Maybe it is for us to be at the right place at the right time to help others. Maybe it means that when someone passes, he or she was about to confront a horrific experience, and therefore God removed the person from facing it.

Perhaps this is just my way of being able to accept things that happen that I don't understand. I don't know. I know that I can see what happened to me, even if it is a small part in this universe, and I know that it indeed changed me. Maybe for the better and maybe not, but I do have a different outlook and one that I probably wouldn't have had otherwise.

The people who were around me made a difference; perhaps that is the key. Maybe it is for all of us to see. Maybe we are all here for each other and we are supposed to do exactly that. Be here for one another.

It says in the Bible that "He" will help us as long as we try to help ourselves. The spirit of the soul is one of the keys to peace. The positive that can be gained from the negative can be our power to behold. It can change attitudes, which changes lives. This attitude control makes our time through the negative seem to move more quickly. It is a release.

So my "negative" started to turn to positive. It was now time for me to be able to stand with my full body cast with the assistance of crutches. The memories of my time on the Hill came back quickly, and there was no need for physical therapy instruction for the use of them. Ha! Were they kidding? I was the master of the sticks! Oh my…I was standing again! It was exciting, and this was a glorious memory for me, one that I welcomed with open arms. It didn't matter how old I was, the room still looked different at this new level just like it did at The Home. Yes…it was another step forward.

Even though I was a master of the sticks, I still needed someone to walk behind me, as my body kept falling backward from being in bed so long. This new level of sorts was an automatic backward fall. Oddly enough, the position of my head was a new adjustment that I didn't anticipate either. I had lifted my head all through the day during the years that I spent in a body cast in bed and when I finally was able to stand up my head kept automatically moving forward, which was why someone had to be behind me. The action that I had to take to stand upright made me fall backward, missing the point of balance, but `I was actually physically walking through doors.

Life in a cast continued with hopes of being healed. Every few months I went to the hospital, had my cast cut off, and had X-rays taken of my leg. Each time, I was rolled into the room and I watched as they sawed off my cast. It was so weird! The blade only cut the cast and not the skin. The cast just broke off into pieces and my body parts beneath it became exposed. The skin looked strange. My left side looked different from my right and my naval always had casting dust inside of it. I just enjoyed seeing two legs side by side, even if it was just for a short bit, as for years the healing had not happened and they would wrap me up again. Another cast, another enclosure that I was unable to escape. My bone just took forever to heal.

Just like my travel to The Home, I still didn't hear the words that I was healed. This cast covered most of my body and it was a protection for me. Soon it started to feel strange without it. This was a different type of "molding." One might think that I would finally give up, but I didn't! I would win and I knew it.

I was conditioned to respond to a negative answer, but I always thought that they would say that I was healed. I continued to believe. As usual, I always thought that my next checkup would be my last. I had mastered my Half-Smile response for so many years that when I didn't need it, my face was blank. I was so surprised! I had tricked my mind so often in order to prepare myself for a negative answer that when they said I was healed I didn't know how to respond. Astonishingly enough, I just was completely quiet for a moment, as in disbelief. I wasn't silent long, as I am sure that everyone within miles could hear me laugh when the reality of their statement finally sunk in. I was moved to the orthopedic floor, and once again, I was put in traction. I wasn't in a children's hospital bed with high bars, and I wasn't on a hard slanted board either like at The Home.

It wasn't even like the attachment of traction that I had after our accident. This time I just had my skinny bare leg placed in a small apparatus like a hammock with a Velcro bandage attached to my ankle with minimal weight. I didn't even have a metal pin through my knee. It felt like my leg was just elevated and quite normal. I thought about what my youngest brother had said to me when I was in the hospital after our accident and I smiled as I thought about how much that statement had helped me to be strong. He said to just close my eyes and exhale through my smile.

This method of changing my attitude worked and I had used it for years, but now, I didn't need it anymore. I could exhale with my eyes wide open and smile easily. My leg was slightly lifted, and so were my spirits. I had my husband by my side. We were celebrating and soon, I would be his walking wife.

Like any new step, my process of starting to bend my knee would be one that would be difficult and slow. I had to practice exercising the bending motion as many times as possible. It didn't want to listen to me just like the time that I tried to make my foot take a step in The Home.

I hadn't bent that knee for so long that it just wouldn't move. I cannot explain how strange it was to see two legs side by side. My muscles had atrophied somewhat during the years of waiting but I knew this building would also take awhile. My smile was real and the Half-Smile Haunting was disappearing.

I didn't sleep very much that first evening. Thoughts of walking were so exciting that it kept me awake. The fact that I would be able to get into water again — just like when I was in The Home — was overwhelming me. Free at last! Yes…I would be submerged in happiness.

Company came and shared time with me during these last few days of being in traction. We had fun, and our joy was penetrating the room. I was healed…again!

I thought that it was also strange that the hair on the leg that had been encased in casting was dark black. I was blonde and when I looked down at my legs, not only were they not the same size, the difference in the shading of the hair made them indeed look like one of them belonged to someone else. I just smiled and knew that they were mine.

I kept practicing bending my knee, and I would be mesmerized at the motion of it moving. I really can't remember how long it was before I noticed that my femur seemed to be bending out to the left side, making it look crooked.

My mind raced with all the medical reasoning for this possible vision. I thought that it was indeed possible that it looked like that only because all of the pressure from the cast that kept my muscles close to the bone for all of those years, and now that they were free, maybe this new shaping was normal. I kept thinking that once I exercised those muscle groups, the proper shape would return. I was just kidding myself, as I knew that something was wrong again. My mind raced with fear and the anticipation of falling backward again.

I called the nurse. I hit that button so many times it was unbelievable. Some people say that when they get very frightened their hair stands up. My heart was pounding fast, and I started to have tears in my eyes.

The nurse finally came in and I asked her to look at my leg. She did. I watched her face as she gazed down at my leg from the side of the bed. She said, "I'll be right back." Her leaving the room seemed a clear indication that something was indeed wrong. I tried to keep my mind from racing, and I tried to use the positive mental defense mechanism that I learned as a child. I kept trying, but this time it was too hard.

She came back into the room with many other nurses who had expressionless faces. They told me that they had to move me onto a stretcher and take me down for X-rays of my femur. I already knew in my heart how they would read. I nodded, as to give my consent, but I wasn't smiling.

They positioned themselves around me and used the flat sheet that was under me as a lifting and moving system to take me from my hospital bed to one on wheels. The moment that they started to move me, I screamed! I asked them to stop and said that something was definitely wrong. I felt like knives were slashing into my bone! They continued to move me. It felt like a million knives madly slashing without stopping over and over again. I kept yelling, "Stop, please! You have to stop now. Just stop for a moment!" They didn't. They finally got me on the stretcher and started out of the room and down the hall.

I continued to scream louder than ever, not thinking or caring about any patients in other rooms. It was as if I was in my own world. The corners were the worst, as it was like the knives moved double and triple time, cutting into my bone! I was crying so hard, and they still would not stop.

Finally they got me into the X-ray room and the motion stopped. The tears were rolling down my cheeks and I could hardly speak. I looked up at the technician and said, "Please do not move me. Please just let me stay still for a moment. PLEASE!" He did! I kissed my hand, reached up, and touched his arm. He knew not to move me.

The X-rays proved that I had a necrotic bone, meaning the death of a bone. I had taught for many years, but I never remember reading about that type of bone. So the X-rays showed that the inside of the bone had not healed, it had died. So...I was not healed after all!

The operation was scheduled. They would graft bone out of my left hip, opposite from the polio hip, and fit it into the femur where needed. They wouldn't actually know how extensive the operation would be until they opened me up.

They explained that they would then put a plate and screws into the femur for support, but that eventually they would remove them when it was totally healed. This was not happy news, but at least it would be finally over. I just could not believe that I had spent all of those years in bed and many years to follow in and out of body casts. I guess it wasn't anyone's fault, just simply bad luck.

The night before the operation, I remember leaving the covers off the left side of my leg that they were going to operate on. They said that they would probably have to slit me open from the knee all the way up past my hipbone. I just wanted to see it looking normal for as long as possible because soon it would be different forever. I wasn't vain. I simply wanted to see it looking normal for a while. The operation went well, and they had to throw away much bone that was mushy. My left leg is an inch and a half shorter now. Lots of mush! I had to be on crutches again for another year, but I had mastered that. They seemed like a part of me. I even had a little purse attached to the crutch on my right to keep things in. I can't remember what was so important to keep in there now.

Another operation and just a few more months with crutches, and then I would finally be walking free. My leg healed, and my scar on my leg meant nothing to me. The scars that I had gained with the years that followed that icy night remained in my soul, but hidden.

I walk without a limp once again, unless I have been standing or walking too long. I was just happy to be walking, so I didn't think about the negative. Of course, I have pain all the time in that area, but I have learned to deal with it. I am still standing today, and I hope there aren't too many challenges yet to face. I have climbed many "steps" already.

I am endlessly grateful for all of the people that have always given me support throughout my challenging times. I consider myself extremely lucky. I will never forget each one of them or the time they shared with me.

I will also never forget all the years that my husband and I slept together in the hospital bed that was placed in my parents' living room. It was our room and our space. I still laugh about how it felt comfortable in that twin-sized bed. Most of the space was filled with my cast, and I am sure that it was not comfortable for him. It was another bonding of our union. At least we were alive and able to share that tiny space. Having him beside me made falling asleep easier, and at the same time I fell more deeply in love.

CHAPTER 8
BIRTHS AND BLESSINGS

CHAPTER EIGHT:
Births and Blessings

We had spent many years living with my parents until the day came for us to move. I was still on crutches but able to manage on my own. The "dark" was now behind us, and the steps into our apartment were easier to climb. I didn't have the weight of that massive cast around me, and we walked into our new home with less weight to carry all around. He opened the door for me, and we started our life together as one over again.

It was a cute apartment and one that, interestingly enough, had a view of the woods in the back. The woods and trees stilled stayed with me like the view from my windows at The Home. It brought me peace.

I remember having to hobble around that apartment with the assistance of my crutches. Sometimes I felt very frustrated because it had been so many years of still trying to heal. I was sick of my sticks, but I found little tricks to make using them easier. I attached a small leather pouch to my right crutch so that I could carry things around with me from one room to another, and I found different ways to use my crutches for support as well.

When I sat down where there wasn't a place to put my leg up in the air, I just put my leg on top of one crutch for support. These methods of managing didn't make the time go quicker, but they calmed my frustration level a bit.

I got stronger as the time passed, and we decided to take another new step into our future. We had been through a traumatic event and we were very grateful that it was starting to be behind us. We found that our love had deepened very quickly while we were traveling through those traumatic times, and we both felt the desire to start a family. Our doors were opening all around us.

The Closing Door

I was healed, and our wish to have a child came true. I carried this little one without a problem, and the extra weight that I carried didn't hurt my leg. I was so happy the entire time I was pregnant. I had gone through two traumatic times in my life, so this event was joyous! After pain I would receive a gift! I would have a new baby who was a perfect mix between the two of us. I remember smiling and laughing throughout my pregnancy, and I even asked my doctor if it would hurt the baby because all I did was laugh. He laughed while he answered my question, as he knew why my happiness was at an all-time high. I was leaving the dark behind me, and soon I would have a new light in my life.

When I was delivering, my husband and I stared at the mirror that was above us and watched as the little head started to be visible. All of the sudden, the head turned to the side, and as if in seconds, the birth was complete. It was a girl! A beautiful, lovely girl. It was a glorious moment and one that I will never forget! My level of pain control was higher than most due to the trauma I had experienced prior. This time when the pain was over, I would receive the most beautiful gift in the world. Thoughts of that alone made the pain manageable.

It was a miracle and we were blessed. She was our own special angel and the sunshine of our lives. We knew that she was a true mixture of us both when the doctor placed her in the tiny baby bed. We watched as she immediately crossed her feet, imitating the actions of her father when he was lying down. Then, to our amazement, she then lifted her small arm and placed it over her eyes as if to block out the light, just like I do. It was amazing and proof that she was ours. She brought light into our lives following those dark days. She slept well and smiled often, making her arrival an easy adjustment. I knew when I looked into her eyes that very first time that she would continue to make me smile and bring me warmth with her presence. I was blessed once again.

Eighteen months later her sister arrived! It was another plan that worked, as God was helping us to be able to move forward once again. The birth was much quicker, but the delivery type was hard. Another beautiful little girl and another bright light to lift our hearts. She would double our happiness! We were so lucky. I kissed her tiny forehead and she smiled back at me. She was a reminder that God will bring us joy and that He will help make the dark parts of life disappear. He will hold us tightly when we need it, and brush up against us when we don't. I received another little "present." This second little girl was another blessing in my life and another reason to believe. She was so beautiful!

They looked like twins, with their blonde hair and blue eyes, and they were always together. It was an easy transition from one to two. They were only eighteen months apart, so they shared the same interests. They played together and laughed often. I prayed at night thanking God for his blessings, and I asked him to please keep them safe from harm. I would be their protector. It was important to me that they would never have anything happen to them like what had happened to me, and I promised myself that I would help all the doors stay open for them.

They had their own rooms but we found them together often. The doors to their rooms never were closed. One night I heard giggling from the baby monitor. It was more than one giggle. I jumped up and ran into our newborn baby's room and there they were, laughing together. Our older daughter had somehow crawled out of her crib and into her sister's room and up into her bed. I was frightened that it happened, but I laughed and envisioned them being friends forever. It was a special bond, and one that I was quite familiar with. They had an important family connection that was a team of love and a team of support. They would be each other's "crutches" when they needed to be.

They went through the same growth as others with happiness mixed with pain. Accidents happened and the healing began, but they were never alone. The bonding continued, and they supported each other along the way. Our house didn't have as many in it as when I grew up, but it was a happy home. We continued to teach them life lessons, and I passed my mother's on. They are sensitive to others and are driven in their own ways. They are different, certainly, and maybe by choice, but the same in many ways. They have never disappointed me in any way and have made me proud.

The Closing Door

I never had terrible twos, fours, or teens. They have only been a joy and a blessing to me, and I kept praying for them to stay healthy, grateful that they didn't have an experience like mine.

They chose different activities of interest and did well in their fields of choice. One was more of a free spirit, the other daughter was more goal driven. I found it is so interesting how they almost automatically were drawn into fields that fit.

Then the nightmare began...

Our oldest daughter often complained that her stomach hurt. These complaints began in her seventh grade year. She would crumble to the floor with pain, and we didn't know why. Many trips to different hospitals and many visits with different types of doctors, and we could not find the answer to her sickness. This went on for years, and during this period I kept praying for her to be healthy. Feelings of my stay at The Home started to haunt me again. As parents, we all know that the most difficult time is the time spent worrying about our children. Not knowing why a child is sick is probably the hardest space for us to be in. When there aren't any answers, it can spin us downward and almost crumble the spirit!

There were so many needles and so many tests. It was ridiculous! I just held her hand and said, "It will be all right, my dear." I was the protector, and I tried to reassure her that someone would figure out what was wrong. At least my parents knew what was wrong with me when I was crippled.

As usual, after a day resting, she was back to school and life would begin until the next time. We referred to these as "attacks," and they would come back again and again. One day, an emergency room doctor came back into her room after her tests and had the answer. He said, "Your daughter has Crohn's disease." We just stared at him and we were silent for a moment. Then my daughter's eyes became very wide and she asked him what that was. He explained, and it all now made sense. It wasn't polio, but it was crippling.

Dee Van Balen

We filled prescriptions and life continued as smoothly as possible. She became even thinner taking all of the different drugs that were prescribed, and it was affecting her so much that the spark in her eyes seemed to be fading. Then one day we found out about a doctor in Jeannette, Pennsylvania, who specialized in this field. We went to see him. He was a gentle soul, and when he spoke you could feel the calm. When he was talking with her, he actually was describing exactly how she had been feeling for years. She couldn't believe it!

As he asked her questions and she answered, it was almost as if he had experienced her years of pain. He continued with the exam and assured her that he would make her healthy again and that we should trust him. Then he turned to face me, put his hands on my shoulders, and he promised me that he would give my daughter back to me. I hugged him and cried. We all cried.

One of the first things we were instructed to do was change her diet. Then we followed all of the natural methods for healing he prescribed. She stopped taking the drugs that were making her so sick instead of making her feel better, and soon she gained a little of the lost weight back and her eyes...her eyes once again started to shine! She had months instead of weeks between these "attacks" now, and life was starting to become a little more normal. The doctor had told her though that there was one section in her abdomen that he was very concerned about, and this was the area to watch. He knew that she refused to go back into the hospital, but he told her that it was very important that she listen to him because that was what emergency rooms were for. Sometimes we need to have those medical procedures and medications.

Then...she was crying so hard and was all curled up in a ball in her bed. I went in and asked her if it was her stomach again and she said yes. I told her we had to go to the emergency room and she refused. It was so scary, as I had never seen her this sick before. I was trained in emergency care but all of my training was not working. She wouldn't listen. I reminded her that the doctor said that in an emergency we had to go! Finally she listened.

The Closing Door

The prognosis was that she had to have emergency surgery. Her colon was about to explode in exactly the same area that we had been watching. This time the doctor said that she would have died if I hadn't brought her. My dear family friend was her surgeon. I trusted him and so did she.

The tubes that ran into her nose after the operation were filled with green liquid. She was so sick and so frail. For two weeks, I slept beside her as my mother had slept beside me. One day her aunt on her father's side came in and changed the mode of healing. Her aunt said, "It is time to get up and shower and start you moving along. You are OK, I promise." She was another nurse by trade like my mother, and she was a great friend. She was also right. It was hard for me as her mother to get her up and moving because I was so afraid of hurting her and witnessing more pain on her face. I guess that I too had almost had enough. I had to be the protector! Sometimes it is hard not to protect!

All that I had hoped and prayed for was for our children not to have any experiences like I did as a child up high on that hill! My prayers were not answered…

But my daughter eventually healed and jumped back into life. She always was a deep-thinking soul and had struggled for so many years with this sickness, frustrated so much until they finally found out what was wrong with her. The "unknown" is always an area for people to be apprehensive and nervous about. It is much easier to deal with a situation when you know why it is happening. So this frail little girl started to look healthy again, following the new diet plan and adjusting her lifestyle for healing. She used her journals as one way to absorb what was happening to her, and this was one venue for her that worked. Releasing her thoughts on paper helped fade the marks that she wanted to go away. Soon the dark, deep passages turned lighter, and this method of managing was her "secret weapon." She is a great soul and gifted with words, and the power behind her work helped her. Maybe one day it will help others too. I love her so much!

We all have our own special ways of managing. The important thing is that we find a way that works! My "personal clock" and cheating time was one of the methods that I used for my own life management high on that hill. I had to find many methods of managing back then because time was my enemy.

During traumas, I knew that my positive attitude and belief in life were what I had learned in The Home, and they were my focus during my years of healing. It was my "secret." I indeed believed that my daughter would get the spark back into her eyes and that her spirit would return, glowing brighter than ever. She had made it through it and now just had to spend her life managing it...this disease called Crohn's.

Being a parent is one of the most beautiful blessings that God gives. It is a feeling that cannot be explained unless you have the opportunity to be one. It is truly a miracle. When our children are faced with any type of stressful situation, it affects us too. Just assuring them that we are with them is a security.

Our youngest daughter has had many challenging times as well. She has been hospitalized with physical injuries and operations that kept her from normal activities. She was an athlete too. Certainly she has also had her heart broken, but the darkest and hardest tests she had to face were the passing of eleven of her friends, all under the age of twenty-five. She has lost many family members as well, and she is not yet thirty years old.

The most painful part of life has to be loss. The grieving that followed my daughter's losses changed her. Many of us have had to face the death of a loved one, and it can be very difficult to recover from this type of trauma. We never forget…but it does get easier.

I believe younger children are overcome by different fears when they are faced with the loss of a loved one. It is written that there are five steps to follow when dealing with death and dying. I think it is a very individualized process and that these "steps" are higher and harder to climb depending on the closeness to the individual.

The Closing Door

Time can be your friend in the healing process, as I have tried to show throughout this book. Other people can make a significant difference in your life. It is the support of family and friends that helped wipe my daughter's tears away from her eyes and helped the sparkle return.

The grieving was dreadful, and she had a very difficult time finding her way out of the sadness. She says she managed to accept what happened only because she knew we loved her and would never leave her side. She is grateful for the support of her family and friends, and she believes that support is what helped her find her way out of the darkness. The darkest of times brought forward another lesson. Out of that trauma was another strengthening of the "family union" — and that was the healing bandage for this break.

She still suffers silently at times when thoughts of her loss slip back into her mind. But she has learned to focus on the positive aspects of life. She will never forget those she lost, but she refuses to let these sorrows rule her life.

Now when she is faced with a challenge she says, "If it weren't this, it would be something else, so let's find a solution." She is a fact-finder now more than ever before. She hopes to become a lawyer, and I feel her drive and desire to seek the truth will make her one of the best! Her heart is big, and the insight that she has gained traveling down these hard roads will push her even harder. Death is still hard for her, but she knows that if her friends have to face loss, she can offer a deeper understanding and hopefully will have the words to help them.

She quotes Josephine Billings: "To the world you may be just one person, but to one person you may be the world." She tells us that we are her world. I tell her she is ours and that I love her very much. Lessons....

I hope anyone who chooses to read my book can look forward and reach out to people who believe in them. It is a power there for the taking. Believe in each other and never step away. Be the "helper and the gardener of the spirit." Believing in someone who is inside of the dark just may be enough to pull them out. It is a support system that works!

To her sister and me, my daughter says in the words of Kobi Yamada, "Thank you for believing in me before I believed in myself." She continues to shine and I am so proud of her. She is my other shining star. Equal to her sister, as they share the same light.

Once again, life unfolds and the value of God, family, and friends lights up the day as they filter into our lives with love and support. The days are brighter now, and we have climbed the steps of closing the bond between us. Wounds will heal and so will hearts with time. Memories we want to erase will fade eventually, but the time traveled with people we love and friends we trust never will.

There isn't anything I wouldn't do for my daughters! Not because of having a commitment simply because I birthed them, but because I love them with all my heart and soul! It is an unwritten rule that does not expire. There isn't a document that simplifies the rules or directions for this parenting either. Reaching out is a must!

As parents we must continue to demonstrate how not to give up in the most challenging times and to reinforce how much we love our children no matter what! That is what is important! The power has to come from within, but the force of the care from others lights the way. The road never seems as challenging with others there to help.

The D.T. Watson Home care has followed me throughout my life. I will never forget, and I will do all that I can to return the care when I can. The place still guides me even as an adult. Yes...sometimes it has led me to have a false hope or outlook, but the path I follow with the positive force that I received there has made the trip much easier to ride.

I cannot tell the story as it has not unfolded as yet, but I will tell you that I still pray to God for assistance in helping me find my way with the "parenting." I know that my children are my blessing and

The Closing Door

I know that without them I would not ever have known the true love and connection that it brings. Children are our shining stars and they are the light that feeds our souls. At least I have always felt that way.

My daughters are the loves of my life and the light within me. This "oneness" is an ongoing growth. All of the time we share builds us. Our friends help build us too, always being there when we need them and, at the same time, we are there for them in times of need. It is a connection of sorts and one that completes our circle of life. It is another secret strength that calms the soul. Moments of life shared with family and friends bring you together and change you for the better.

Both of our daughters are strong! They have an inner strength that to this day amazes me. I love them both with all of my heart and I feel confident that they will continue to follow the proper light that will lead them to secure love and personal peace. My older daughter is a strong woman with great insight to life and love as well as the world around her. She will move mountains with her words and light the paths for many to follow.

My younger daughter has conquered much darkness too and has conquered harder ground than many. She has the inner strength to rise above and will indeed be successful too in her endeavors. She has traveled her own star of sorts, arriving at the center of self. She is a gifted soul and one that will fire up the world, too.

They will both find the *life light* because they will be *the match that lights it*!

So while our own family walks down our paths of life I feel confident that we will continue to have each other to lean on and to share life's blessings as well as the clouds that decide to hover for a while over one of our heads. I have tried to give them the grounding that they needed to be strong when faced with adversity and the awareness of having an open heart to give and receive love. I have tried to instill upon them the importance of caring for others. It is important to care for the people that care for you. This is a valuable lesson, as life is too long not to pay attention!

Life has been filled with much more joy and happiness in our lives than any kind of darkness that we have had to face. The deep love that we share is one that is overwhelmingly great and all of the times that we have gone through together both good and bad have been the steps that got us to our "oneness." Our happy moments in time outscore the dark moments. Our smiles are real, and our hearts are happy. We all know that there are paths yet to follow, but we know that we can face them and win. A map of life... our centering is *us*! My daughters have turned their dark times into *flowers of life*! They are the *flowers* that are unique and stand tall and out on their own. They are confident and they have learned hard lessons and made these moments "*books of flowers.*" Just like one of my mother's favorite verses from May Sarton's "The Invocation to Kali," my girls are indeed "...the always hopeful/Gardeners of the spirit/Who know that without darkness/Nothing comes to birth/As without light/Nothing flowers."

So our "family dance" continues to be fun and our time together a treasure. We will face all challenges without fear, as we know our love is strong and we have each other. We recognize the beauty of life, we listen to the songs of the birds, and we know that the sun truly continues to shine brightly!

CHAPTER 9
SLAMMING DOORS

CHAPTER NINE:
Slamming Doors

The title I chose for this book stemmed from the impact that my vacuum-pressured door had on me in that Children's Home high up on that hill. It was the most vivid memory that I took from the entire experience! The title doesn't mean that doors always close but rather that they open with new beginnings. It wasn't the door as much as what stood in front of it and what was left behind. So many meanings in one! They are the windows and doorways to the mind and they can be the root to mastering life. Doors close but they open too and with them, anything is possible. I am still working on which way to open or close my personal doors, but I welcome the event of choice and I continue to choose the one that brightens my view and lets in the light.

I never even thought about a door until I lived there! Now…it is my haunting. It is a haunting of many emotions. I didn't understand how many meanings could be analyzed from the memories of that door closing and locking me in alone. After traveled through time I recognize all of the multiple meanings that affect my heart and affect my soul about my "CLOSING DOOR."

Yes, doors close and doors open. They come in many sizes and shapes. They fit into specific openings and they have locks. At the top of our body is the "key" to opening and closing all "doors"! My closing door now is my opening! What started out as a nightmare ended up my awakening! I have the key and I can open any door!

I have based my love and attention, even though it is for all not just one, on my sweet mother. She is and always will be my own special blessing. Everyone has a special connection to her in my family. Even my daughters still hold her high in honor and love. They were young when she passed and it hasn't been the same since she died. I still feel her presence.

The Closing Door

My door slammed shut the day she died! She was my pillar of strength and the one who helped open all of my different doors to life. She was my true friend and the greatest mother that anyone in this world could ever dream of. She was beautiful and had a heart of gold. She was my queen and the person that I hoped to mold myself after. The day that we found out she had cancer was like a shocking horror story! Not our mother! She had helped so many people throughout her life and now she faced a possible death. She chose to use the "Half-Smile Haunting"! She would beat it!

I never thought about any other path that we might have to take! Remember? Steps were for climbing not for standing on! I never even had a conversation with her about the fact that she would not live, just as she never had one with me the entire time I was in the Watson Home. I would walk and she would live! Period!

Mother continued to follow the plans that the doctors suggested in order to heal. We moved the hospital bed back into the living room of their home just where my parents placed me after we returned home from our accident. I made the room comfortable, dresser and all. Now I was the caregiver and she was the patient. She did much better than I did, always smiling and being positive. She could stand for only a few seconds until she didn't have the strength to continue. Time passed and her weakness increased. Her positive attitude stayed strong though and her eyes let you know that she was still fighting. She was strong in her mind and wouldn't give up! Another lesson, I guess. She continued to be my "Master of Life"!

My sister was a nurse just like my mother, flew home often, and helped so much. She was my rock! Our other sister lived very far away but managed to join us along with all the rest of the members of my family to help Mom. My mother's six children and their wonderful families were all there. My father was in denial and that was that. He could not accept the fact that she had cancer and might pass away. I don't know what I would have done without my family beside me. My husband loved her deeply too and was very supportive. It was hard on us all watching her suffer.

She kept smiling through it all and we laughed often. Her doctors were fantastic and we had hope. I never knew what my mother was really thinking but a little later I found out some of her thoughts from my baby sister. I guess it was easier talking to my sister since she too was a nurse. Maybe they look at things like this differently than we do...

The life lessons never cease. I learned a lot from it all as well as did others. I saw another venue of sickness throughout the cancer halls. Hope on the faces of those who suffered told another story. They had their own story. It was a story that you could almost feel without a word being spoken. They had a bond with others in their field of pain and disease but they all seemed to have a fresh sparkle in their eyes and a new outlook on life. So positive and directed! Wow...

Isn't it amazing to think about all of the people that have their own stories to tell? So many stories! The fact that some people don't ever stop to listen simply blows me away. Our senior citizens have knowledge that would enable us to have a cushioned future if we would only listen. I mean it isn't as if all of the people that I know do not pay attention, but the reality of it all is that too many people do not. It is almost like those people that don't choose to listen keep their doors closed, locking out life.

One of the most powerful life lessons that I had happen to me during my mother's sickness was the day I came to the hospital after teaching and I opened HER door and peeked in with a smile. She had one of those head wraps on and of course smiled back at me with such strength. Not the strength of muscle but strength of soul and self! A woman of many talents and a woman that indeed our God put here for a purpose! She was a saint and a giver. A lady that at all costs would be our pillar of strength for all to lean on. Her love was never ending!

Here is the lesson. I crawled up into her hospital bed and started to ask her how she was doing and I continued taking the conversation away from the tubes that were attached to her. It had been a day

The Closing Door

since I was with her but she was easy to talk to and the time spent sharing was easy.

As I sat with her, filling the time with stories of my day, I told her that my pointer finger hurt because I got a paper cut during one of my classes. Before the entire statement came out of my mouth, I looked up into her eyes horrified that I would even tell her something like that when she was laying there getting chemotherapy. She rubbed my arm ever so gently, as she always did, and said softly, "Oh, I know, those paper cuts really hurt. It's OK." It was as if to say that life still continues and the pain of others is still real. A master of life this sweet mother of mine.

That same day I had asked my father to go to my house and take care of our puppy and that I would stay with Mom. My husband had the kids and therefore I could. He did and when he got home, he took a nap on the sofa. He positioned himself as he usually did and took his hearing aids out and put them on the butler's table while he slept. When he awakened, the hearing aids were not there. We searched everywhere and the final deduction was that the dog had ingested them! The vet checked her out and she was fine but we still never found the hearing aids. We laughed because after this happened we used to say that this wonderful little puppy still didn't listen.

Time passed and we all took care of Mom. She was slipping and even though the time had arrived, I still believed! The doctor said that she would have only about three more days to live. She was struggling to breathe and her chest sunk in deeply as she took each breath. I called everyone that wasn't at the house yet and told them to identify themselves and tell her that they loved her as she was failing. The last person that I called was her mother. Granny was strong and my mother smiled as her mother spoke to her for the last time. I don't know what she said to her, but I am sure that it was spiritual. My father was the last to speak to her before she went into that coma state. I never got my chance. I seemed to have used my "fake blocking" as I did in the Children's Home about losing this person in my life. It was almost as if she would be back and was only on vacation. I don't think that this method of managing was working this time.

One of my older brothers and I sat in the kitchen to have a coffee. My nurse sister was in with my mother and all of a sudden she spoke in a loud voice for us to come in. I stared at her face as if I had never stared before, almost like trying to have her hear what I was thinking. Please, Mom...

She took her last breath. The moment was a nightmare. No...no... no...I thought, *it isn't possible*! I still continued to believe, and even though she was still, I wasn't giving up. I called 911.

I am sure that there are many people that have been through this, as there isn't anything much worse than losing a loved one. I'll never forget them zipping her up in that black bag and rolling her down our sidewalk and into the ambulance. It is a vision that will shake me every time I think about it. I have reached down inside my soul for all of the life lessons that I have learned to help me forget that tragic moment. I still remember...

The days passed and the family that she raised knitted closer together more than ever. We found a note that she had written many years before she got sick and I had it framed. I wonder if she secretly knew then. I will never have that answer.

I was worried about how my father would do without my mother with him. I was surprised that he stayed strong and kept the calmness. He still calls me daily and I love him dearly. I am indeed very lucky!

The room was unbelievable! It was Christmastime and the flowers surrounding her were brilliant. The flowers were everywhere. They were lined up halfway up the walls in the room and down the hallway. It was beautiful and so was she. There wasn't any pain on her face any more. She looked absolutely stunning. She was indeed a queen and the flowers and people that surrounded her demonstrated the fact. The number of people that came to show their

The Closing Door

respect was more than I could ever have hoped for. Indeed, she was loved even more than I had imagined.

Her mother was strong and kept everyone strong. She too was the master! It wasn't long before she left us after Mom died. The two of them were great powers in this world. Many lessons were learned from these two brilliant ladies. I am certain that they are together now watching over us all.

My mother has been so much of an influence on me throughout my entire life, so much so that I have dedicated this book to her. My Master of Life. Watching her leave my bedside at night in The Home was the most devastating experience that I have ever had. "THE CLOSING DOOR."- Now she would be gone forever. I feel strongly that each night she sends her kisses and they fall gently on my eyelids. I still feel her with me to this day. I know that she knows I loved her and that I will continue to climb the steps of life with her in my heart.

We all had a very hard time accepting the fact that our mother was no longer with us. She had been our strength and our leader. We knew that she felt confident in the fact that we would all continue to take care of each other without her present, as this was one of the main lessons that she had taught us all.

So time changed paths again and we all managed to adapt to it. I found myself trying to fit in her shoes, so to speak, and continue her place in the family. I tried to fill the void that was impossible to fill, as this woman was not a match to anyone. She was the guiding light and the force behind all of us. I tried. We all tried.

I wasn't prepared for what was going to start happening to me in life next. My "Time in a Bottle" seemed to be starting to crack. This man that I loved seemed to be starting to disappear. It was a shocking new path and one that was hard to understand or follow. Silence started to enter my life. A new void of sorts just started to slip into my marriage. I tried to keep the door open, but as the time went on it seemed to be closing. Closing in on me and starting to shut me out. That damn door!

Words came easily to me my entire life. I could always read people and it was always easy to understand how they were feeling. Many times they didn't even have to say anything. I just knew. I don't know if it is a gift or a curse, but I felt confident in my ability. I knew that this ability also was something I had learned while I was in The Home. I was sensitive to others.

The perfect couple was now not so perfect. No one knew when it first started or even for months afterward. I didn't even know why. No bond is perfect. We had our differences, just like everyone else, so it didn't make any sense. No matter how hard I tried, I failed. I used every method I could think of to have this man of mine respond, but I couldn't. I didn't give up, as that was not who I was. I believed and that was that. This "slamming of doors," so to speak, would pass. I waited for the calm to set in. It never did.

For the first time in my life, I couldn't adjust my thinking. All of my secret methods of managing weren't working. Those magical sealing words were not heard. He refused to say them. So I went for a very long time not hearing them. "I love you." They were the only three words that I ever needed to hear. I believed in love and I needed to hear those words. I just didn't understand. Why were we together if those words weren't felt? Did it mean he didn't love me? Anyone would say of course not. Did I have a curse from the Hill? Or was it just a fake feeling that people are sincere about caring? I was so confused. The thought of it all sickened me. No matter who was wrong or who was right, we were supposed to be together. Or were we? I know I was not the one who gave up.

He was my magical man and my shining knight. My love of my life wasn't there anymore. My heart began to break, piece by piece, until I had a hard time keeping track of the pieces. I knew this puzzle, or so I thought. This man was my other half. What in the hell was happening? I tried to keep the trauma from our daughters, but later I found out that I wasn't all that successful. I guess children's ears are larger and more powerful than they look.

I thought about all of the time we had spent together and how it seemed impossible for this to be happening. We had traveled many paths of happiness, and we were a stronger couple after our accident. We had two beautiful daughters who depended on us. It was a lot to give up.

I had waited for years to be healed twice in my life. My medical managing was easy compared to this matter of the heart. This type of waiting was exhausting, and it was breaking my spirit.

My life had always been centered and based on truth and on believing in all people. But because I am a "heart" person, I need the reinforcement that indeed I am correct! I needed to be loved because I love unconditionally. The three "magical words" were a major factor in my being. It wasn't much to ask.

We sat at the kitchen table discussing the situation, and I asked him to see a counselor with me. It was important not to give up on a lifetime together. I knew that we had different opinions on some life topics, but no matter who was right or who was wrong it wasn't a reason to give up. I had never given up on anything in my life. It was important to keep this union together. I was shocked at his non-emotion and at his response. He was not willing.

The conversation continued but I won't share what was said, as it is private. I will only say that those words *made* my door close and that I *had to leave it behind me.*

CHAPTER 10
HILL STREET CLIMBING…

CHAPTER TEN:
Hill Street Climbing

It wasn't long before we found a place to live. I had to make a quick exit, and it was one of the most traumatic things I had ever done. I will never forget it. After what I had just experienced, this move should have made me happy to leave it behind. But it didn't.

My parents always taught us not to accept less than we deserved. That at all costs, be true to ourselves, and to believe in all of the good that life has to offer. I didn't feel that I deserved what had happened to me or that I should be the one to make any step in the direction of healing. I was done, but I didn't give up.

Hill Street...713 Hill Street...Wow! This time my "Hill" climb was not to mend my leg, but to mend my heart! It was a new climbing of sorts. This new space was not far from the "Hill" where I learned many lessons as a child. The "Hill." It was the place where I learned to walk again and now I was learning to walk on a different path without crutches.

My steps were just as hard, as my heart was what was in need of mending. Strange, isn't it? Our new address was also the date of our wedding! I didn't even know it when I signed that contract. I had been so upset about being in the position that I was in that I didn't notice until the morning after I signed that sheet of paper. It was ridiculous and it made me feel sad. 713...I still can't believe it. I just kept thinking that 713 would be like a new start. I would start over and I would make sure that this time I would not be hurt. I would control who would enter my world and take all of the steps that I could to protect myself.

We made it cute, this new home of ours. It was big enough for the three of us, certainly not like what we were all used to, but it was ours. I vowed to continue trying to be a perfect parent and I knew that it would be hard. I wanted to make sure that I could protect my daughters and I tried to keep the security within our walls.

The Closing Door

I tried to hide my pain and to smile often. Smiling was always easy for me, but now it was forced like the Half Smile. Yes, another haunting had begun. I was placing one brick at a time. I wasn't able to control this new "ticking of the clock" and my new window took awhile for the birds to sing me good morning songs. Now I was on a personal roller coaster. This emotional life track was speeding up and then slowing down with time. I wanted to smash my clock.

Therefore, the steps to get into our home were many and climbing them each night after work was hard. Not physically hard, just hard. It was a door that was hard to walk through. It was a new life in another world. But I knew that my secret power from the other "Hill" would find its way back into my mind and mend me.

The world that we left had been fun, until the "change." They grew up in a loving, kind home. We were always there sharing life and making special memories together as one. I would say that happiness filled our home most of the time and that life was actually grand, even if it was only in my own mind. We had gone through so many years of hospital visits after our accident and we had enjoyed the life that we were building together. Our home was beautiful and we loved our daughters. I used to erase any memories that hurt but now it was more difficult.

These feelings sweep over me today as I realize that this inner outlook of "It will be OK," a term my daughters think I cloned, was my calm. But the statement "It will be OK" was my magic now. It was another new way of "mind management." My positive outlook that I learned up high on the "Hill" as a little girl was now coming back into effect! I would be OK, and we would all be OK! Now I was starting to be back in charge of my heart. Time was healing and time was up. Time was being wasted waiting for the man that owned my heart to come to me. But he never came and he never called. His heart was his own now, so I believed. He was traveling down a road now of his choice. He gave up by choice.

How does one move forward when the past is still haunting? Almost a lifetime had already been built and then the building stopped.

The answers never came as to why it all happened and that made it hard to get over. Why? I understood that when I had polio I had a reason to wait, and I think that I did a great job while I was waiting. This time I didn't have a reason to accept. This time I was stuck in the "unknown," and that is an area that none of us like to be in. If only I had an answer it would have been different.

We look into a mirror and we see the face in front of us. My oldest brother always said if people would look into a mirror first then maybe they would see the problem and fix it. Look to yourself first. I did. I stared in the mirror but the answer didn't come.

I see clearly now but I AM STILL CLIMBING…

This new change and climbing was definitely not something that we planned. My daughters and I had to climb together and as we did, the steps became easier. We continued to adjust and get used to our new surroundings. They continued going in and out of the door but without any slamming. We started to find a re-birthing of our bond and a new connection. They were older now and our level of communication had changed. They were scholars it seemed, finding the right words to say to change the mood. They even seemed to understand life better than I did at times and knew when it was time for a hug. A silent hug, and one that took the pain away and replaced it with peace.

So we were protecting each other. I remember looking into their eyes when they were born and I knew that I would always love them unconditionally. I would make all of my decisions in life with their best interests at heart. I knew that this change would affect them emotionally. A heart should be protected at all times. Sometimes I think that I hovered too much trying to make sure that I blocked any scars from developing. We laugh about it now.

Communication is another key. It is the key to most things in life. We talked daily, but I guarded how much I discussed with them, as I didn't want them to have anything else to worry about. They knew that I had tried and I am sure that they saw the change coming quicker than I did.

The Closing Door

Regardless of any wrongdoing, we were a family, and this separation was difficult. Mixed emotions were definitely shared by each of us, but we kept the lines of communication open and it started to heal our hearts.

I felt like I needed to protect myself from ever being hurt again so I started to build a wall of protection in my mind, and my heart assisted in the building. My children say that I was a wreck emotionally, but I felt strong inside of my mind. I could still see the light through the clouds even if others didn't notice that I did. The change was difficult but I knew that I could do it. I just tried not to travel back into time that would reopen the wounds that I was trying to leave behind.

My daughters were my focus and my support system, and my family unit that helped me through it all. We were all proud of each other and the light started to shine brighter on our home. The love that you receive as a child is a blessing. I believe that the moment that your parent picks you up you immediately start to feel it. When you wrap a baby up tightly and hold him or her in your arms, you can feel the baby's calm. The baby feels protected. That is a parent's role. We are immediately committed to automatically love and protect our children. I was so lucky to be loved and so lucky to have had the parents that I did. They gave me deep roots and wings to fly when I got older. Their doors were always open, and I knew that I could re-enter them whenever I wanted to.

So this protection is comforting. Now I felt the need to protect myself. I had to protect myself from any more pain as I started to rebuild my life. Just like the extension of a family that the staff up high on the "Hill" was to me, they protected me too. I felt safe there. I was lonely, but safe. I knew that I had to be there and so I let them give care and I was grateful for it. There are always people around you that can help with protecting when you need it.

Well I know that some people do not succeed in the rebuilding but I knew that I had enough love from the people around me to make it through it all. My youngest sister, remember the one that got stuck on the towrope skiing? Well…I tried to reach out and help her during that dreadful night up high on the slope and failed. The mystery man didn't though, and during these long hard years of life she has been my "mystery man." She could climb up any pole to handle any trauma. She is the queen of results and healing power! She has given me hope when I was out of it. She has been the other partner or parent for my children during this transition. She loves them deeply and has worked very hard to be a positive force that stands beside them. She has always enjoyed time spent with them, and has shared some of the "life pain" with them. New life paths have a way of making new beginnings.

We have discussed the power of the mind. We have reviewed venues of success within self that are used as defense mechanisms for inner peace. We have discussed how people or situations affect our outlook and ability to adjust to the level of calm within. The reality of what is and the ability to adapt to it is how we can move from one place in life to another. My older sister has also been another light to me when I feel lost. She is a light that has given me new direction because she was with me. She is a star that shines brightly for all of us and one that somehow manages to gently cause calm within all of our hearts. Her voice and her words are powerful yet very soft. She can turn the light on for anyone who feels lost in the dark. She is one of the most grounding people that I know and I am blessed to have her for my sweet sister. She has always had a special spiritual connection and I admire her for her ability to have such unwavering belief in the power that we can all receive from above. She knows that he is in charge and she trusts that he will always be the force that will lead all of us to safety. She is right. Her encouraging words of wisdom are magical and her presence is my gift and my peace.

She would tell me that I had to change how I thought and change the things that I was used to doing. Step into the future and adjust your attitude. Hum...change. It is funny but I did and the first thing I changed was the position that I fell asleep in. It wasn't easy at first but soon the position felt comfortable. Time went on and I continued to find my way through the darkness. I knew that I could make this new direction in life exciting and fresh. It was a new beginning.

The Closing Door

My wall was becoming stronger. Building, building and building. One brick at a time.

I quit teaching because I obtained a patent on a product that I invented. It was a product that would make a difference. "SIGHT SHEET" is an attachable visual aid that magnifies print and can be used as a promotional item. For years I had been trying to move this product into the mass market, but my "direction change" didn't allow me the time. I had been working on rebuilding my family life and I was determined to rebuild my professional life.

Much time passed, and the passion I have for other things in my life has helped to dim the light and the hope I held in my heart for my husband. I continue to lift bricks, but it has become easier. Other lights have filtered in and out of my life, changing my view and opening my mind to a brighter future once again but they were easier to lift because I had closure.

As strong as I have become, I recognize that the lack of closure with my marriage and my husband is what still gives me pause. But non-closure is an ugly space between smiles.

I have met many people who have been negatively affected by a perceived lack of closure. Having a reason is closure. Not having a reason is traumatic. But I've come to realize that for some, trying to slip away so they don't have to face a challenge is the reason why a final conversation is avoided. Or maybe it is just the calm they feel in the space of "oneness," and that space is safe, and they are not willing to go back.

The unfortunate side effects of these types of actions are the scars that are left behind for the parties who seek closure. These wounds heal very slowly, but they do heal. The "bricks" that must be lifted to rebuild end up being very heavy, but they can be lifted. And you must lift them.

We all have the power to will the good to us. We all can decide which space we want to fill. Leaving the past behind sometimes is very hard, but we must take the good that we got from it and move on. It is hard, but we can do it. We all manage to find our way with time. Time heals all, they say. We must fill in the cracks of our lives with faith. If and when we cannot fill the cracks, then we must learn to step over them.

We all have many blessings that we can be thankful for. My children give me joy and they fill my time and space perfectly. I believe that my children are my light and I am blessed having them by my side. They will never know how much I actually love them, because I cannot put that level of love into words.

I know that they feel my love and that they will continue to walk forward individually with the strength of many. I am proud of the adults that they have become and they have grown along with me in matters of the heart. They are believers too and our bond is a connection of the heart that is like a circle. The circle does not have an opening for others to enter without permission and a private sort of shape that is our mark in time. I love them more than life itself, as they are my other part of me. They know that my love is unconditional and they have my love without trying to get it. It is a magnificent power and a blessing, this circle of ours.

I know that they will be successful in their lives. They have hearts of gold and they realize the importance of life. Both have been down hard roads of testing and have survived. Both have experiences of their own that have given them different outlooks toward life and love. I pray that they continue to build their own special bond, as someday I will not be in their physical circle of love. However, I have assured them that I will never be far away. I will make sure that I give them signs, when I am at rest, to let them know that I am still with them. I am confident that they have all the knowledge and skills they need to find any conclusion.

For my sweet daughters:

The Whole of Life
By Pat Whelchel
Age is a garden of memories
Flowers we plant on the way.

The Closing Door

> And the dewdrops we see on the roses,
> Were the tears in some far yesterday.
> Age is a tall slender willow,
> Lending its song to the air;
> And if one small branch is yellowed,
> It dims not the beauty that's there.
> Age is a book we have treasured,
> If one little flyleaf is torn.
> Age is a cool shady pathway
> That winds by a murmuring brook.
> If one small portion is rocky,
> It's just a detour we took.
> Your garden is filled with the flowers
> Of all the kindness you've shown.
> Each blossom looks up with the sweetness
> Of all of the friends you have known.
> The pathway you walk has been gladdened,
> The song of the brook is more clear.
> The whole of life has been brightened.
> Because of your presence here.

> Remember…
> Life isn't measured by the number of breaths we take, but by the moments that take our breath away. I LOVE YOU!

Life continues to amaze me! Every day is a new story. All I know is that I truly just want everyone in this world to be happy. I pray that their crossroads of challenge are minimal and I hope that each of them has people that touch their lives and their souls for the better.

It is important to hold in your heart the knowledge that sometimes the disappointments that we experience in life are just that…"disappointments." They are NOT the Spirit Breakers of our souls, but rather the positive forces that guide us to where WE need to be in this life. They build our character and the education along the way shows us a different route or personal path for brighter futures. It lights the way…

It is indeed interesting exactly how many times one must change, though. I am finding the knowledge and strength to once again return to the center of "Me." We all have moments that force us to go back to the self. Remolding and rebuilding is a must, but we can shape it.

I try to stay on the positive path of believing and bringing my "Santa" into each new day. I try to find the light that clears my vision and find the power to analyze, correct, and move on. I know that I share in the pain anyone who realizes that a union of sorts doesn't work. I know that the ramifications of realizing what we thought was right wasn't really right at all. I will strive to have the power to continue to make that damn door open. I will design my own door and while I am designing it. I will learn to adjust anything that isn't a proper fit. I know that designing my own door is ongoing and that it takes skill. I will make it swing open on command and close when I want it to. I will also design the key as uniquely as the door so that it fits snugly and follows my command in the direction that I want it to turn. We all have life experiences that make our "doors" not a proper fit, but it is important to learn from all of the moments of the making and adjust accordingly.

"THE CLOSING DOOR" was my opening. I had the key all along. My travel from The Home gave me a tremendous start to designing my door and the "CLOSING DOOR" never really closed. It is still the force behind me that helps me open the doors that are around me. My mother is the key to that door and I will continue to use that magical key until the day I die. It is my strength and I will continue to use it as I continue to travel through time.

CHAPTER 11
A BLESSING OR A CURSE

CHAPTER ELEVEN:
A Blessing or a Curse

We said our blessing before dinner. We held hands as we prayed and in that prayer, as it always was, were the wishes of peace, happiness, hope, and good health for all. I didn't feel well during dinner. I had never felt that way before and I never have taken a nap in the afternoon. That day I did.

I awakened with pain in my abdomen and pain in my chest! There was an odd feeling that seemed familiar to me. Fright filled my body and I jumped up out of bed and walked around in my bedroom for a moment. The pain wasn't going away...oh God, please not something else! I tried to get back into bed and relax, telling myself that this new episode was NOT real! Thoughts of dying swiftly entered my head and rolled around in my brain with no way out! No, no, no! Not now! This cannot be happening to me. I have had enough. What? Then that old cliché of "What doesn't kill you will only make you stronger" popped into my head. Enough is enough! I had taught CPR, lifeguarding, standard first aid and had used my knowledge while I taught school and ran swimming pools most of my professional life! I knew what was happening to me and it scared me to death!

I also knew what that strange feeling was in my abdomen. I knew that this familiar feeling was indeed a blood clot. I had been hospitalized twice in my life for blood clots and had been on blood thinners for years; therefore, I knew what was happening to me.

I said to myself that I would just get dressed and drive myself to the hospital. I didn't want to awaken my daughters and frighten them. I mean, they certainly had already been through enough with me. I could do it myself. But...I couldn't.

I walked into the closest bedroom of one of my daughters and said that she had to get up and immediately take me to the hospital. I said we couldn't call an ambulance because I was sure that I had a traveling blood clot and we didn't have time. We needed to leave immediately! I was so scared!

We walked down the steps and I told them where all of my personal information was listed, like my life insurance information and bank accounts, etc. While I was hovering over the information, I had to lean over and hold the table for support. I truly thought that I was going to die. We left.

I walked into the hospital and they started to ask me questions. My daughter answered them for me. The nurse told my daughter to register me and for me to follow her. Was she kidding? I had taught first aid, and I knew I shouldn't be walking. She disappeared into a room for employees, and I turned back around and sat on a chair. I thought I was going to die! Flashes of my life passed through my brain, and I was so angry that I was having another physical medical experience! How could God have let this happen again?

The nurse came back out and said to follow her. She led me to a group room and told me to put on the robe, and then she shut the curtain and left me! It wasn't a vacuum-pressured door. It wasn't any type of door that closed, it was just a curtain. But the moment that the curtain closed, fear welled up in me, and I screamed for my daughter! Another door was closing!

I don't remember much after that, and I couldn't even think about finding my special "key" to open the door. I knew that I had IVs inserted into my arm and that I was being transported by ambulance to a hospital thirty minutes away that specialized in pulmonary medicine. My wonderful daughters were there and alongside of them was my special goddaughter and my best friends Mae and RD. Having them with me should have been enough power to make me heal immediately!

I truly was not in a great state of mind, and I couldn't even concentrate. All I kept thinking was, "Not again!"

Now if anyone has experience being a patient, it is me! More than one-third of my life had been spent being just that! This time though, I was not a good patient at all! I felt that life was unfair and that it was just impossible for anything else to be physically wrong with me. I wanted to run out. I wanted to not be there with needles in my arms and a hospital blanket over me again. No. I will not stay for a third time!

Flashes of memories exploded in my mind. It was like a lifelong time capsule that quickly showed flashes of my past before me. In a moment, I saw myself in The Home struggling with polio and then having a hard cast covering me after our accident. Pictures of my family and all the feelings connected to them flashed in my mind like a movie. It was so fast! How could all of this be a "flash"? Time…wrapped up in a moment. A quick reminder of life's experiences all rolled up into one thought in an instant. Isn't that strange? It makes me wonder about all the stories people tell about what happens when you are about to die, and that thought crossed my mind as well. Was I going to die? I saw my mother's face…

This time I was very angry, and my daughters told me that the only thing that I didn't do was have my head turn around on my neck! I couldn't help it. I had morphine drugs in me, but it didn't matter. I was NOT GOING TO GO THROUGH THIS AGAIN! ENOUGH IS ENOUGH! NO MORE HOSPITALS FOR ME! But I stayed…

I remember the doctor coming into my room and very clinically starting to explain what had happened to me. I just stared at him with "my" blank look as he kept speaking in his monotone voice. He could tell that I really didn't want to listen to him. It was obvious that I was angry that I was in the hospital again, even though he had no idea how often I had been a patient in my life. So he just stopped talking for a moment. Then he said, "I can tell that you don't really want to listen to me right now and that you want me to go." I said yes.

I healed and there was no permanent damage to my heart. I will always have to take medicine to thin my blood, since I missed this blood clot. I still cannot believe that this happened to me and sometimes, to this day, I feel like I am reliving that moment when I looked at that doctor with the blank stare. By the way, how is it possible that some people **never** even have been in a hospital?

The Closing Door

I thanked God and we, God and I, had another private discussion about life. He is my friend and knows me well. We talk all the time, although he is probably tired of listening to me. I know that he will continue to give me, and all of us, the strength that we need when we need it. I haven't concentrated on the fact that another door closed on me and I, once again attribute that to my "Closing Door" lessons. At times, I think about what type of door would fit into this scenario and I visualize one that is shattered. Those damn doors!

A blessing or a curse...

I have referred to my experience on the Hill as a blessing. Not a blessing that I would wish on anyone, and certainly not one that I would have asked for. But it happened and my mind takes me to only the results that were a positive part of it. A molding of a solid spirit!

The blessings were many. I have found that intertwined with this blessing are many characteristics of my personality and outlook on life that have been a curse. I am NOT anyone special, and I have never thought that I was. I know that many people in this world have their own stories that are life shattering. I know that I am only a small seed in the flowering. I am writing my story because it is my story alone. It is a story that I hope will help others to believe. It is a story that I hope will help others see that their situations are a blessing and not a curse. I have grown to realize that my blessings are plentiful and that my attitude has been adjusted because of it.

When I say that maybe it has also been a curse it is because I have visualized life through flowered glasses. My glasses were shaped because of my past. I know that I don't see some of the realities of life like others. I am slow to see the negative. I believe in all people when I shouldn't. I have traveled through time with an attitude that was based on what life is. A world that is beautiful and a world that can give us all that we need. A world where love is real and caring is too. I am challenged when others don't see it too. It is very hard for me when I watch people be disrespectful to one another. It is unacceptable to me for anyone not to go out of his or her way for others. I think that it is ridiculous when people fail to believe! Santa is alive! The positive will surpass the negative!

So when I question the battle between the "blessing" and the "curse," it is just that. I finally accepted that fact that not all people get it and that is why my blessing will not be my curse. I will fall with the inability to see people for who they really are in situations of the heart. I will pick myself up and move on with my "attitude" adjusted for self!

The negative energy that shades our lives can be adjusted too. I will continue to try to give to others and to look for the love just like the love that I obtained from my family and from all of those that were with me up high on the "Hill." It is self-owned and, yes, sometimes "self-destructive," but I recognize the ability for it to be a curse so I will fight it. I will continue to try to make a difference. I will not allow this "curse" to affect my pattern of thought or to fit in any way into my "puzzle of life." It may bring me down, but I won't stay there. I will pick myself up with the help of my "crutches," and move toward the light!

I will continue to TRY to be a light for all others. I know that I am NOT anyone special and I know that my force within myself to make a difference will one day help someone. People have helped me throughout my life and it is with their guidance and building of my spirit that I am grateful. They made life bright for me and they put the flowers into my glasses. They planted the seed for me to grow and I am only trying to give back by writing the lessons that they gave to me. It is they...not me.

They have helped me climb higher steps in life and if not for them, my moments of managing would have been harder. They instilled in me the "magical thinking" that has enabled me to believe stronger than most. That was my blessing. The curse is only the moments of allowing the shadowing of negative into my mind that stop me from being able to open doors and break my spirit. The power that I gained from my "CLOSING DOOR" keeps me reaching for the positive and keeps my spirit strong.

The Closing Door

Every day I meet someone who inspires me. This world is full of people with different stories that make them who they are. I have found that some people do not choose to take the time to listen or to share with others. Those that pay attention to others gain from the experience and have magnificent stories of their own that are a result of taking the time. I believe in life and all of the good that is out there for the taking. I believe, even when I have no reason to, that there is hope behind all of the gray clouds and closed doors. This may seem unrealistic to some, and that is where my time on the Hill conflicts, but it is how I truly believe. My "Closing Door" was a blessing.

I know that my family and God changed the path of my life. I know that even though my road has had sharp turns that I wish did not happen they did, and I will continue to search for the happy part of the light that guides me. I will never forget to thank others and I will always be grateful for all of the steps that I have had to walk along the way because I have managed to climb them. WE MUST ALWAYS BELIEVE!

We can choose to fall deeply into the negative. As my mother used to say, there are those who will choose to blow out others' candles in order to light their own. But those who do will not be able to have the peace in their hearts while they are traveling with that attitude and belief. I am amazed at all of the people that do not have the opportunity to be blessed with having as great a support system as I have had. They had to do it on their own! I admire these people the most, for they found the light blindly. They had the deepest conviction of belief. I would love to read their stories.

So I must keep believing and not allow myself to think about a "curse" because indeed it was a BLESSING! Each one of us can decide how to make the choices of "Managing Moments."

I will continue to strive to stay on my path that was prepared for me to follow. I will continue to strive to make a difference in this world, even when mine is crumbling. I will pick up the pieces with the help of my loved ones and friends and all of those who care to share life with me. I believe in life and even though my "Time in a

Bottle" turned upside down, I will spin it and pick it up and let the light that is before me shine through it like never before. I will win!

We can all find great people in every part of our lives. I have been lucky, as many people that I have not made reference to are deeply engrained in my heart as beautiful souls. They are another "secret power." They touch my life in a positive way and have enabled me to make it through all of my own challenges. I thank all of them for that. Even my friend that groomed our dog has a special place in my heart and it will stay there strong forever. It is funny because she always says that she doesn't believe in God. Ha! She is more like God wants us to be than most…that silly lady! She will see eventually. She was another blessing to me.

So my curse is just that. It is a piece of the puzzle that I still try to lose because it doesn't fit. This negative part of my "blessing" is just that. It is a part of the realities of life that I continue to fight and fix.

I don't have all of the answers, but when it comes to the heart I do. We all need to see the positive and we all need to help erase any negative that comes to us and stand by each other when the confusion begins and not let the "curse" take over. We are not alone.

So this "muddled state of sorts" is challenging. It doesn't enable us to be the so-called always-hopeful gardeners of the spirit. Who knows that without darkness nothing comes to birth? As without light nothing flowers." Which flower will you choose?

Being a "gardener of the spirit" is to care about others and to communicate that to one another. If you know someone cares, life is sweeter. Having a person in your life who truly cares is a blessing in itself, as with this comes a light that is brighter. It is a "dance" of the souls. But sometimes other people make that too difficult, don't they? It isn't hard to communicate. In fact, it is easy. Good communication is the key to peace. It can bring the calm to any unsettling space. But when a mind isn't open and a heart is closed there isn't much you can do but continue to have faith and hope and…keep trying. Like the Serenity Prayer….accept what you cannot change. I want to add to that prayer. I want to add, BUT KEEP THE FAITH!

The Closing Door

> Life and love is like a rock...HARD TO BREAK.

This passage from my mother's journal, a poem called "Children Learn What They Live" by Dorothy Law Nolte, says it all:

If a child lives with criticism,
He learns to condemn.
If a child lives with hostility,
He learns to fight.
If a child lives with ridicule,
He learns to be shy.
If a child lives with shame,
He learns to feel guilty.
If a child lives with tolerance,
He learns to be patient.
If a child lives with encouragement,
He learns confidence.
If a child lives with praise,
He learns to appreciate.
If a child lives with fairness,
He learns justice.
If a child lives with security,
He learns to have faith.
If a child lives with approval,
He learns to like himself.
If a child lives with acceptance and friendship,
He learns to find love in the world.

> As Beverly Sills said, "There are no shortcuts to anyplace worth going."

CHAPTER 12
THE OPEN GLASS DOOR

CHAPTER TWELVE:
The Open Glass Door

I wonder sometimes if things happen simply because they are a coincidence or if situations occur because they were meant to be. I introduced my roommate to her husband over twenty years ago and I met his parents and his older brother. Much to my amazement I was having dinner in a restaurant one evening and I heard a couple in the booth next to me mention a name that was familiar to me. It so happened that they said he was the chief executive officer of what is now called the Watson Institute! I was shocked to say the least! How could it be possible that someone that I hadn't seen for so many years was actually in charge of where I lived as a patient? Not only that, but he obviously shared in the value as well as the mission of the institute! Wow!

The next day I gave him a call and we chatted as though only a few weeks had passed since we last spoke to one another. His name is Mr. Raymond B. White. He was shocked to find out that I had lived there and had written a book about how the experience had changed me. Coincidence? I don't think so.

I told him that for years I had driven up that long hill to sit outside of the closed section that used to be the entrance, just to sit and think. I told him that it always made me remember to be strong. This touched him and he surprised me by arranging for me to step inside the closed section!

I had always wished to have the opportunity to go into the Watson Home and he made my dream come true. I cannot put into words how excited I was. The fact that I was going to be able to tour the inside of the D.T. Watson Home for the first time since I'd left at age six was unbelievable!

The date was set and I drove up that long hill, this time with extra speed. I couldn't wait to see Ray again but I was overwhelmed thinking about walking down the halls of the old hospital.

The Closing Door

The original road had been closed off for years so I had to drive a distance down and around the new section to get to it. I sat outside waiting for Ray to arrive, but he didn't come. I got concerned and called his office only to find out that he was waiting for me at the new entrance. I laughed and started to drive back around the wooded drive toward the correct destination and I was still smiling.

I drove up and there he was looking just as I had remembered him! We hugged for a moment and he introduced me to a few of his co-workers that were going on the tour with us. We walked inside of the new entrance and I was thinking about the fact that I wasn't wearing a brace and I didn't have crutches!

We started to chat and he was giving me information about all of the additions that were made to The Home since long ago. It was beautiful.

I told him that I was excited to see the part of the hospital where I lived and he said that we would go there through the hallways. I looked at him confused because I didn't understand. The old entrance was very far away.

I had just driven that distance. I told him that it was impossible. For just a moment I thought that maybe I had been wrong all of the years that I had driven up there just to adjust my attitude.

We walked down many halls and I shared part of my personal story with him. As we walked, I still felt odd inside that my "entrance," wasn't really my entrance. All of a sudden, we turned a corner and I found myself in the hall where I took my first step as a young child! It was phenomenal! Tears came to my eyes and I told him that I was standing on the very spot that I did when my foot finally listened to me and moved just a bit! I could smell the magnificent expensive wood that held much history in it. I was right! What I didn't know was that behind all of the trees and past the hill the new section was connected to the old. This made the visit for me more magnificent than it would have been if we had driven around and entered the original entrance of The Home where I had sat in my car!

It sent chills down my spine, and I took a step.

Our tour continued and it was fascinating to revisit the inside of The Home. We walked into the Grand Ballroom where I had I slept the night before Christmas. It was unbelievable. I looked out of the window and smiled, thinking how I tried to count the falling snowflakes. This Grand Room looked smaller since I was taller.

Some of the rooms had changed, and the pool that was the second step to my therapy was no longer there. He pointed out where everything used to be and it was all so familiar. I was back in time but in an adult body. We walked over to the elevator that my mother had ridden for that long year and tears started to come to my eyes. Then he pushed the elevator button to go up to the floor where all of us "little people" lived. The anticipation of stepping onto the floor and walking down the hallway in my heels was overwhelming. Then the doors opened.

I stood still for a moment when we stepped out of the elevator and just looked around. I needed a moment to think about all of the time that I spent on that floor and how my stay had affected me. I didn't share everything that I was thinking.

I had spent my time inside of a room, so the hallway felt as if I had been there before, but I wanted to step into my room. We walked down the hallway and I opened a door on the right. I wanted to see if the room was just as I had remembered it to be all of these years. It was, and I got chills down my spine and all over my body standing there. It was my own "tiny room" and my tears that streamed from my eyes were not from the size but from the education that I had there.

My tiny room was a life course filled with lessons that would never leave me. Again, tears started to come to my eyes. I tried to hide the fact that I was so emotionally touched by the moment, but they witnessed it.

My magical window was exactly where I had remembered but the birds outside singing were not. I smiled as I remembered it all with a happy heart and I chuckled when I looked at the floor where I had crawled out of my bed to try and walk the night the "mean nurse" was on. What a mistake that was. But the tiny blessing of hope that I received from my roommate's smile when I tried to take a step was one of the most powerful experiences that I had ever had there. It was a mark in time! I believed even though it didn't work and I knew I would keep on trying.

Then my emotion of strength changed drastically as I turned my head to the right in exactly the same direction that I did each night when my mother was leaving. "THE CLOSING DOOR" that stole my mother from me and for a moment I felt alone again. That damn door! I guess that is another example of my reference to "HAUNTING…"

My time on the hill…so much of me is still there.

Ray and I sat in a conference room for a long time looking at old photos of the land and the home that David and Margaret Watson built and owned more than one hundred years ago. His passion for the Institute and all of its history was very visible in his words and expression. His knowledge was very extensive and I was so proud of him. I was also amazed that he was so deeply connected, but I didn't find it odd. We shared a deep passion for the Institute and he never even lived there. This was a man that found his place in life. He was another builder and a man that would keep the true meaning of the D.T. Watson Home alive. He is indeed the perfect person to hold that position, and I know that he will protect it and continue to fulfill the "Watson Dream." He too is making a difference, a Watson difference!

The Watson Institute's mission is as follows:

> The Watson Institute, through its family of schools and services, helps children and youth with special needs to achieve their fullest potential in all aspects of their lives. Watson strives to provide programs that serve the needs of children with autism spectrum disorders, neurological impairments, or serious emotional challenges with diagnostic, educational, and

therapeutic support; support to the families of these children through education, counseling, wraparound, outpatient services, and respite programs; and training and technical support to educators, psychologists, therapists, and others working in this field.

My story continues to build with life and the people that I love and care for. There are certainly many chapters to come that are not written yet and I look forward to following my path that is in front of me. My time traveled to the "now" has been my personal road map to discovery. I have spent much time analyzing life and being grateful to all of those whom I have met along the way that touched my life. This chapter titled the "Glass Door" is just that. It is the door that you can see through. It is a door that many other people may find a connection with in some way or another. I decided to open this door because I know how much all of the people that have walked with me during this journey so far have helped me. It is my way of saying thank you!

Now it is time to close my door. I have exposed my deepest feelings in order to demonstrate how an experience and the reaction to it has affected me. "My" experience up high on that hill so far away from home changed me and I am so grateful for it! Maybe that is where the saying, "Home away from home" started. At least for me it did...

I still believe, and sometimes it amazes me, but I know that life is beautiful and I am happy to be a part of it. The leaves still dance with the music of the wind, and the birds still sing their own special songs. I hope that you chose to open the doors of your heart and your doors of choice. Step outside and let the sunshine radiate your soul.

It is a beautiful world!

CHAPTER 13
YET TO COME

Chapter 13:
Yet to Come

The title of this chapter is "Yet to Come" because as I have mentioned, I do not know what paths are ahead of me. Once again, this book is just "my story." I was going to leave this chapter open because of not knowing what lies ahead of me. This chapter was supposed to be blank.

But someone asked me why I wrote this and I looked at him with sincerity and explained that without my family and people who reached out to help me throughout my life travels, they would not have ended as they did. I told him that it is hard to pull out of the dark when you fall and that it is other people that lift you out into the light.

Yes…we can do it on our own, but sometimes it is hard to stay lifted and that is when people can reach toward you and pull you up. I even find times when I have to re-read my own book when dark clouds hover over me. We all need to be reminded and all of us can stay bright. Some of these words may be redundant, but isn't life? The saying, "If it isn't one thing it is another," is so true. A strong attitude helps us glide through it.

So…for all of you who I have mentioned and to those of you who I have not, thank you for walking with me. You have made a difference in my life. My eyes are wide open and my "door" hasn't been heavy. It is because of all of you that my door swings open easily. Because of you, the light breeze that touches my face makes me smile. The sections of my life marked by you made those "Doors" beautiful and they opened without pushing on them. It has been like magic.

We can all shape our destiny and bring the goodness into our lives with these "lessons" that are shared.

The Closing Door

I stated that any "Door" that I would open I would open now by choice. It took years to get back to this centering of self and the dark doors of my past seem to be fading away. I can still see their shapes and colors, but I cannot visualize the trauma marks that used to be boldly engrained in them.

Now....I do not need a key and the lessons that I learned from others and the lessons I learned at the D.T. Watson Home for Crippled Children are my guide. I do not know where this new chapter will take me, but I am excited to greet each new day with a smile on my face and light in my heart.

The following poem will encapsulate my feelings and my thoughts, as well as my hope that all people find their happy light and hang on to the loving care they receive from others. Notice little things in the beauty of nature, as these God-given beauties can be a special tool for lifting your spirits. Watch for them!

Butterflies remind me of my mother. Ever since she passed away, it seems as though they fly around me when I am thinking about her or when I need to be lifted myself. They inspired me to write the following poem:

Butterflies
Is it a feeling deep inside?
Is it a true measure of beauty that changes form like life?
Is it the test of time and waiting?
Can we see its beauty?
Can we feel the way that it lifts us?

Can we catch it to touch it?
Can we keep our eyes on it as it flutters by with grace?
Can we for just a moment have it land on us?
Do we take the time to take in its colors?
Is it a secret gift to us that when we do see one it makes us smile?
Do I keep on believing in its strength?
I do believe.
It scares me to think that the fact that it changes and I pray that how I feel doesn't.

Dee Van Balen

It is odd that I have such strong feelings about this intricate, delicate part of life.
It makes me calm and peaceful when I see one.
It reassures me that life is beautiful.
It makes me feel as if it can lift gray clouds that might be hovering over me.
I watch this natural beauty and it renews my faith and positive attitude.
Butterflies are free!
So I will hope that it lands on me.
I cannot control its flight, or its change,
but I can control how I look at this butterfly and life.
I can also control how I feel inside when I see one.
It is like magic.

It makes me feel safe and its beauty reflects back into my inner self,
allowing me to bring it forward into my life.
This tiny beauty assists me in my ability to have faith.
This exquisite creature is my secret friend.
My mother helps it to fly, I think, and I will always be there to watch for it.
I know that she is behind many of the beautiful things that happen here on earth.
I know that she is watching me too.
I believe in how I feel.
I believe in butterflies.
I hope that you do too.

ACKNOWLEDGEMENTS:

To Ashley and Breean: I don't know what I would do without you, my lovely daughters. You have been amazing to me. I will always think of "Landslide" by Stevie Nicks as our song. Keep that song in your hearts as a reminder of our love for one another. I will always be your safety net for all of your "landslides" and there to catch you if you ever fall. I love you both, and I am so proud of you. Remember to laugh often and smile always, and may God keep you always in the palms of his hands. I love you!

To my father, I thank you for being my rock and for loving me unconditionally. Without you, our loving mother, and our family, this story would have had a different ending. To my brothers and sisters, you have been a tremendous support system in all of my "times of need." Three of you were "Polio Pioneers," who made a historical mark in the difference that the polio vaccine made on this world. All of you have been my "crutches." For Gretchen, Karen, and Jan, many thanks for helping me put the finishing touches on this book.

During the final editing of my book, I faced another of life's hardest challenge. My dear father passed away just a few days before his ninety-third birthday. I have struggled with the words to express how his death has affected me. It was a crushing loss, and as I held him in my arms, I know he felt the depth of my love. He too was a light in my life, and I know that he and my mother are together, smiling down on us. The circle of life continues…

Other than my wonderful family, I would also like to extend heartfelt thanks to Sally Mae, Megan, and Nancy for their unwavering friendship and their valuable assistance with the editing of this book of "LIFE."

It is with great respect that I extend my thanks to my special friend and editor, Gretel Gaal Egan. She is one of the most responsible, intelligent individuals that I have ever known, and I so admired her ability to multitask between family and profession and take the

The Closing Door

time to edit for me. I trust her implicitly, and she was so in tune with this story that before I verbalized my thoughts, she spoke my words. It has been a pleasure to share this endeavor with her, and I am grateful for her expertise and time. But more than that, I am grateful for her friendship throughout the years. She was with us while my mother was sick and was a tremendous help managing life for all of us back then. She continues to shine as her life unfolds, and I wish her many blessings.

I would also like to thank all who worked at the D.T. Watson Home for Crippled Children and those who helped me. And I would be remiss if I didn't mention the two great men who opened doors for so many: thank you, Dr. Salk and D.T. Watson!

To all of those who have touched my life and traveled this path with me, and for all of you who have chosen to read and share my story, may God bless you and keep you in his hands, protected always.

As inspirational author Robert Collier once stated, "You can do anything you think you can. This knowledge is literally the gift of the gods, for through it you can solve every human problem. It should make of you an incurable optimist. It is the open door."

> I leave you with this final message: "The sun will always shine through any cloud and *new doors always open!*"

ABOUT THE AUTHOR

Dee Van Balen is a mother, author, inventor, and teacher. A graduate of West Virginia University, Dee taught physical education, health, and science for more than twenty-five years and was a springboard diving coach for more than twenty years. She holds a patent for the SIGHT SHEET® Vision System, a magnification aid and promotional product. Dee also has more than twenty years of experience as a CPR, standard first aid, and lifeguarding instructor. She is currently helping to manage a family-run business. She and her daughters make their home in Pittsburgh, Pennsylvania.

ABOUT THE EDITOR

Gretel Gaal Egan has been working as a writer and editor since 1996. She is a graduate of Carnegie Mellon University with a double major in Professional Writing and Creative Writing and is currently working as a freelance marketing specialist. In what seems like a previous lifetime, Gretel was the captain of Dee's diving team. She lives with her husband and two children in Pittsburgh, Pennsylvania.

LaVergne, TN USA
20 February 2011
217250LV00007B/129/P